The Joy of Strawberries

by Theresa Millang

Adventure Publications, Inc.
Cambridge, Minnesota

Thank you.

A special thank you goes to my friends and all other contributors to this collection. I have included all my favorite recipes using fresh, frozen, canned and dried strawberries. So, pick a recipe and enjoy!

Book and Cover Design by Jonathan Norberg

10 9 8 7 6 5 4 3 2 1

Copyright 2007 by Theresa Nell Millang
Published by Adventure Publications, Inc.
820 Cleveland Street South
Cambridge, Minnesota 55008
1-800-678-7006
www.adventurepublications.net
All rights reserved
Printed in China
ISBN-13: 978-1-59193-168-3
ISBN-10: 1-59193-168-1

Table of Contents

DESSERTS

FROZEN DESSERTS

JAMS AND CONSERVE

MEALS PAIRED WITH STRAWBERRIES

PIES

SALADS AND SOUPS

Gelatin Salads

Other Salads

Soups

SAUCES, SYRUPS AND CONDIMENTS

Sauces

Syrups

Condiments

SHORTCAKES, COFFEECAKES AND CUPCAKES

Shortcakes

Coffeecakes

Strawberry History and Lore

Strawberries have a long and fascinating history. Indigenous to both the northern and southern hemispheres, these delicious members of the rose family have been providing humans with healthy, delicious treats for more than 2,000 years.

The early Romans believed that strawberries relieved symptoms of melancholy, fainting, inflammations, fevers, kidney stones, infections, bad breath, gout and diseases of the blood, liver and spleen. Written accounts by the Roman Senator Cato date back to between 234–149 B.C., and American Indians were already eating strawberries when Columbus arrived.

Early strawberries were wild plants, not the large, plump specimens we enjoy today. The first detailed accounts of strawberry production, including pest control and soil selection were produced in 1697. The first strawberry hybrid developed in the United States, the "Hudson," made its debut in 1780.

Around 1831, strawberries began to be sold at a London marketplace. As they gained popularity in England and Europe, strawberry patches became a familiar sight in the gardens of common folk and aristocrats alike. In the United States, Cincinnati, Ohio, growers became the first to ship strawberries using refrigeration, in the form of ice placed on top of the strawberry boxes.

Today, strawberries are grown in every U.S. state and Canadian province. An extremely versatile fruit, they are used fresh, frozen, canned or dried, in everything from jams to strawberry shortcake and in countless other recipes.

Not all of the attraction involves eating. Madame Tallien, a prominent figure in the court of the Emperor Napoleon Bonaparte, was famous for bathing in the juice of fresh strawberries. She used 22 pounds per basin! Even today, a variety of inedible products ranging from soaps and perfumes to candles and air fresheners carry strawberry fragrance. And legend has it that if you break a double strawberry in half and share it with a member of the opposite sex, you will fall in love with each other.

Health Benefits of Strawberries

Strawberries are not only delicious, they are full of nutrients. Ounce for ounce they contain more vitamin C than citrus fruit, and are an excellent source of vitamin K and manganese, dietary fiber, iodine, potassium, folate, riboflavin, vitamins B5 and B6, omega-3 fatty acids, magnesium and copper.

Strawberries are low in calories and fat-free with less than 60 calories per cup.

They are also a rich source of phenols led by anthocyanins, which serves as a potent antioxidant. Antioxidants have been shown to help protect cell structures in the body and prevent oxygen damage in the internal organs. Strawberries' phenol content makes them defenders of the heart, cancer fighters and anti-inflammatory agents—all in one delicious package!

In studies using animals, researchers have found that strawberries help protect the brain from oxidative stress and may reduce the effects of age-related declines in brain function. They have also discovered that feeding aging rats strawberry-rich diets improved both their learning capacity and motor skills.

Strawberry Fun Facts

- The biggest strawberry on record weighed 8.17 ounces.

- Arkansas, Arizona and California have towns named Strawberry.

- It would take 7 billion strawberries to fill the Titanic.

- There are an average of 200 seeds on an average strawberry.

- The strawberry is the only fruit with the seeds on the outside of the fruit.

- California produces 75% of the U.S. strawberry crop—available January through November, with peak quality and supply from March to May. Florida ranks second.

Selection and Storage

If you pick your own strawberries, be sure the cap remains on the strawberry by pinching the stem of the berry between the thumb and forefinger. This will prevent damage to the fruit and the plant.

When selecting store-bought strawberries, look for firm, bright red berries with fresh green caps, and be sure there are no signs of mold. If one berry is moldy, the mold spores will likely have traveled throughout the package.

Store fresh, unwashed strawberries in the refrigerator; do not remove the caps. Strawberries lose moisture when the caps are removed. Washing tends to bruise the berries and makes them lose freshness. For best results, place strawberries in a shallow container and keep at 35°. When ready to use, place them in a strainer and rinse with cold water. Gently twist off the caps or use the point of a knife.

To freeze whole strawberries, gently wash and pat dry. You can remove the cap and stem or leave them intact, depending on what you will do with them once thawed. Arrange the berries in a single layer on a flat pan or baking sheet and place in the freezer. Once frozen, transfer the strawberries to a heavy food-storage plastic bag, and return to freezer; they will keep up to one year. Adding a bit of fresh lemon juice will help to preserve their color. Strawberries can be frozen whole, cut or crushed. However, they will retain a higher level of vitamin C if left whole.

Weights and Measures

1 basket = 1 pint strawberries
1 pint = 3¼ cups whole strawberries
1 pint = 2¼ cups sliced strawberries
1 pint = 1⅔ cups pureed strawberries
1 cup = about 4 ounces strawberries
1 pint = about 12 very large stemmed strawberries to about 36 small
20 ounces frozen strawberries = about 4 cups whole fresh strawberries

Growing Strawberries

Strawberries are a perfect fit for the home garden. They require relatively little growing space and produce quickly. Each plant may yield up to one quart of fruit during its first season, and 25 plants will normally produce enough strawberries for the average family.

June-bearing, everbearing and day-neutral are common types of strawberries. June-bearing varieties produce during a two- to three-week period in the spring or early summer. Everbearers will produce two or three harvests per season, while day-neutrals bear fruit all season long. Growing strawberries that ripen at different times can provide a longer picking season.

Strawberries should have well-drained soil rich in organic matter. Pick a spot with at least six hours of full sun per day. Do not plant strawberries where peppers, tomatoes, eggplants and potatoes have been grown, as these plants could have a verticillium wilt, a serious strawberry disease. Strawberries need about one inch of water per week during the growing season.

Have your soil tested before planting (contact your local USDA Extension office for help, if needed), and apply lime or fertilizer as needed. Do not fertilize plants during flowering or fruit production, as the berries will tend to be softer and of poorer quality and will not keep well; fertilize early each spring before the plants produce flowers. If you choose the June-bearing strawberries, you could spread another fertilizer application after they have finished producing fruit for the season.

Sources: http://ohioline.osu.edu/hyg-fact/1000/1424.html (accessed 1/3/07); www.urbanext.uiuc.edu/strawberries/growing.html (accessed 1/3/07); http://ohio line.osu.edu/hyg-fact/3000/3012.html (accessed 1/3/07).

Appetizers

FLUFFY CREAM CHEESE DIP

Choose ripe strawberries for this delicious appetizer.

1 8-ounce package cream cheese, softened
2 cups powdered sugar
2 teaspoons pure vanilla extract
½ cup whipping cream, whipped
fresh whole strawberries, cleaned

Beat cream cheese in a bowl with an electric mixer on medium speed. Beat in powdered sugar and vanilla extract until fluffy. Fold in whipped cream. Serve with strawberries. Refrigerate leftovers.

Variation: Stir in 1 tablespoon finely grated lemon or orange rind.

Makes 3 cups.

SOUR CREAM FRUIT DIP

Add other fresh fruit when serving, if desired.

2 cups dairy sour cream
½ cup powdered sugar
⅛ teaspoon ground allspice
¼ cup sweetened flaked coconut, toasted
2 teaspoons freshly grated orange rind

fresh whole strawberries
fresh apple slices

Whisk sour cream, powdered sugar and allspice in a bowl until smooth. Stir in coconut and grated orange. Cover and refrigerate 1 hour before serving. Serve with strawberries and apple slices. Refrigerate leftovers.

Makes 2 cups.

SPRING ROLLS WITH STRAWBERRY DIPPING SAUCE

A special appetizer.

Dipping Sauce
½ cup sliced fresh strawberries
2 tablespoons rice vinegar
1 tablespoon Asian sesame oil
1 tablespoon granulated sugar
2 teaspoons Vietnamese fish sauce
½ teaspoon chili flakes

Rolls
¾ pound cooked shelled shrimp
¾ teaspoon seasoned rice vinegar
8 spring roll wrappers
16 mint leaves
16 cilantro sprigs
¾ cup quartered fresh
   strawberries
1 cup peeled, seeded cucumber cut
   into 2x⅛-inch strips

Dipping Sauce: Puree all ingredients except chili flakes in a blender until smooth. Stir in chili flakes; set aside.

Rolls: Mix shrimp with rice vinegar in a bowl; set aside.

Dip wrappers into boiling hot water for a few seconds until soft; blot on a clean kitchen towel to remove excess water. Place 2 mint leaves, 2 cilantro sprigs, 3 pieces strawberries, 3 shrimps and 3 cucumber strips in a line down center of each wrapper. Fold bottom over filling, fold in sides and roll up tightly.

Serve each roll with 1 tablespoon dipping sauce. Serve immediately or place rolls on a baking tray in a single layer; cover with plastic food wrap. Refrigerate up to 4 hours before serving. Refrigerate any leftovers.

Makes 8 servings.

Bars
Squares
Cookies

ALMOND STRAWBERRY BARS

Strawberry preserves are used in these delicious bars.

Crust
1¼ cups all-purpose flour
½ cup butter
⅓ cup brown sugar, packed

Topping
½ cup powdered sugar
½ teaspoon almond extract
2 teaspoons fresh orange juice

Filling
¾ cup strawberry preserves
½ cup all-purpose flour
½ cup brown sugar, packed
¼ cup butter, softened
½ teaspoon almond extract

Preheat oven to 350°.
Grease and flour an 8-inch square baking pan.

Crust: Beat all crust ingredients with an electric mixer in a bowl until coarse crumbs form. Press mixture on bottom of prepared pan. Bake 20 minutes or until edges are lightly browned. Remove from oven.

Filling: Spread strawberry preserves to within ⅛ inch from edge of hot crust. Beat remaining filling ingredients in a small bowl on low speed until mixed; sprinkle over strawberry preserves. Return to oven; bake 20–25 minutes or until edges are lightly browned. Cool completely in pan.

Topping: Mix all topping ingredients in a small bowl; drizzle over bars.

Makes 3 dozen.

BIG BATCH STRAWBERRY BARS

Good bar for when the gang gets together.

1 cup butter or margarine, softened
1½ cups granulated sugar
2 eggs
1 teaspoon pure vanilla extract
1 teaspoon freshly grated lemon peel

3¼ cups all-purpose flour, divided
¾ cups slivered almonds, chopped
1 teaspoon baking powder
½ teaspoon salt
1 12-ounce jar strawberry preserves

Preheat oven to 350°.
Grease a 15x10x1-inch-baking pan.

Beat butter and sugar in a large mixer bowl until creamy. Beat in eggs,
one at a time. Beat in vanilla extract and lemon peel.

Mix 3 cups flour, almonds, baking powder and salt in another bowl until
blended; gradually add to creamed mixture until mixture resembles coarse
crumbs, do not over mix. Reserve 1 cup of mixture. Press remaining mixture
into pan. Spread with preserves to within ¼-inch of edges.

Mix ¼ cup flour with reserved crumbly mixture in a bowl; sprinkle over
preserves. Bake 20–25 minutes or until lightly browned. Cool in pan on
a wire rack. Cut into bars. Refrigerate leftovers.

Makes 3 dozen.

CHOCOLATE STRAWBERRY SHORTBREAD BARS

Offer this low-fat shortbread bar with a cup of tea.

4 tablespoons solid margarine
½ cup granulated sugar
1 egg white

1¼ cups all-purpose flour
¼ cup unsweetened cocoa powder
¾ teaspoon cream of tartar
½ teaspoon baking soda
⅛ teaspoon salt

½ cup strawberry all-fruit spread

Topping
⅓ cup white chocolate chips
½ teaspoon solid shortening (do
 not use butter or margarine)

Preheat oven to 375°.
Lightly spray a 13x9x2-inch baking pan with vegetable cooking spray.

Beat margarine and sugar with an electric mixer in a medium bowl until
well blended. Beat in egg white until blended.

Mix flour, cocoa, cream of tartar, baking soda and salt in a bowl. Add
to creamed mixture, beating well. Gently press mixture onto bottom of
prepared pan. Bake just until set, about 10–12 minutes. Remove from
oven; cool completely in pan on a wire rack.

Spread evenly with strawberry all-fruit spread.

Topping: Melt white chocolate chips with solid shortening. Drizzle over
cooled bars. Cut into bars when set. Refrigerate leftovers.

Makes 3 dozen.

23

CREAMY STRAWBERRY BROWNIE BARS

A brownie mix is used in this strawberry cream cheese bar.

1 19-ounce package brownie mix
2¼ cups quick-cooking oats, uncooked
1 cup butter, melted, cooled slightly

2 8-ounce packages cream cheese, softened
1¼ cups strawberry jam, divided
2 large eggs
1 teaspoon pure vanilla extract

Preheat oven to 350°.
Grease bottom of a 13x9x2-inch baking pan.

Stir brownie mix, quick-cooking oats and melted butter just until moistened.
Reserve half of mixture. Press remaining mixture into prepared pan.

Beat cream cheese and ½ cup jam in a mixer bowl on medium speed until
smooth. Beat in eggs and vanilla extract until blended. Spread mixture over
mixture in pan. Spoon remaining jam in small amounts evenly over filling.
Sprinkle with reserved brownie mixture. Press down gently.

Bake about 30–34 minutes or until topping is firm and center is just set.
Cool completely in pan on a wire rack. Chill well. Store in refrigerator.

Makes 24 bars.

LEMON-STRAWBERRY BARS

Dust cooled bars with powdered sugar, if desired.

Crust
1 cup all-purpose flour
¼ cup powdered sugar
½ cup butter, softened

Filling
3 tablespoons all-purpose flour
½ cup granulated sugar
¼ teaspoon salt

½ cup whole milk
3 egg yolks, slightly beaten
1 large lemon, including zest and juice
½ teaspoon pure vanilla extract
1 pint fresh strawberries, sliced

Preheat oven to 350°.

Crust: Mix flour and powdered sugar in a mixer bowl. Add butter; beat with an electric mixer on low speed until well blended. Press mixture firmly onto bottom and up ½-inch up sides of an ungreased 8-inch square baking pan. Bake 20 minutes. Remove from oven.

Filling: Mix flour, sugar and salt in a medium saucepan.
Mix milk, egg yolks, lemon zest and juice in a small bowl; gradually add to saucepan mixture. Cook over medium heat, stirring constantly until mixture thickens, about 5 minutes. Stir in vanilla and strawberries; spread over baked crust. Return to oven. Bake until filling is set, about 30 minutes. Cool in pan. Cut into bars. Refrigerate leftovers.

Makes 16 bars.

NO-BAKE GELATIN-TOPPED STRAWBERRY CHEESECAKE BARS

Only the crust in baked.

40 vanilla wafer cookies, crushed
½ cup granulated sugar, divided
5 tablespoons butter, melted

2 8-ounce packages cream cheese, softened
½ teaspoon pure vanilla extract
1 8-ounce container frozen nondairy whipped topping, thawed

1 large ripe banana, sliced
2 cups sliced strawberries

¾ cup boiling water
1 4-serving size package lemon flavored gelatin
1 cup ice cubes

Preheat oven to 350°.

Mix cookie crumbs, ¼ cup sugar and butter in a bowl until blended; press mixture firmly onto bottom of a 13x9x2-inch baking pan. Bake until lightly browned 5–8 minutes. Remove from oven; cool completely.

Beat cream cheese and ¼ cup sugar in a mixer bowl; beat with an electric mixer until blended. Stir in vanilla extract and whipped topping. Spread mixture over cooled crust. Top with banana slices and strawberries.

Stir boiling water into gelatin in a bowl until completely dissolved. Stir in ice cubes until completely melted. Pour mixture over fruit. Refrigerate until firm, about 1 hour. Cut into bars. Refrigerate leftovers.

Makes 24 servings.

STRAWBERRY BARS

Share a bar with a friend.

1 cup all-purpose flour
1 cup uncooked quick-cooking oats
½ cup butter or margarine, softened
⅓ cup light brown sugar
¼ teaspoon baking powder
⅛ teaspoon salt
¾ cup strawberry jam

Preheat oven to 350°.
Grease an 8x8-inch square baking pan.

Mix all ingredients except strawberry jam in a large bowl. Press 2 cups of mixture into prepared pan. Spread evenly with strawberry jam. Spread remaining mixture over jam, pressing down lightly. Bake 25 minutes. Remove from oven; cool in pan 20 minutes. Cut into bars.

Makes 12 bars.

STRAWBERRY-RHUBARB BARS

Unsweetened frozen rhubarb may be used if fresh is not available.

Filling
1½ cups fresh rhubarb,
    cut into 1-inch pieces
1½ cups sliced fresh strawberries
1 tablespoon fresh lemon juice
½ cup granulated sugar
2 tablespoons cornstarch

Crust
1½ cups all-purpose flour
1½ cups uncooked
    quick-cooking oats
1 cup brown sugar, packed
¾ cup butter, softened
½ teaspoon baking soda
¼ teaspoon salt

Topping
1 cup powdered sugar
2 tablespoons fresh orange juice (approximately)
½ teaspoon pure vanilla extract

Filling: Place rhubarb, strawberries and lemon juice in a 2-quart saucepan. Cover and cook over medium heat, stirring occasionally, until fruit is tender, about 8 minutes. Mix granulated sugar and cornstarch in a small bowl; stir into fruit mixture, cooking and stirring until mixture boils and mixture is thickened. Remove from heat; set aside.

Preheat oven to 350°.
Grease a 13x9-inch baking pan.

Crust: Mix all crust ingredients in a large mixer bowl. Beat on low speed until mixture forms coarse crumbs. Reserve 1½ cups crumb mixture. Press remaining mixture onto bottom of prepared pan. Spread filling over crust. Sprinkle with reserved crumb mixture. Bake 30–35 minutes or until golden brown. Remove from oven. Cool completely.

Topping: Mix all topping ingredients in a small bowl until blended. Drizzle over cooled bars. Cut into bars. Refrigerate leftovers.

Makes 36 bars.

CHUNKY CHOCOLATE STRAWBERRY SQUARES

Hint: To speed cooling, refrigerate 30 minutes.

1½ cups all-purpose flour
1½ cups oat meal, uncooked
½ cup granulated sugar
½ cup brown sugar, packed
1 teaspoon baking powder
¼ teaspoon salt
1 cup butter or margarine, softened
¾ cup strawberry preserves
1¾ cups semi-sweet chocolate chunks (11 ounces)
¼ cup chopped nuts

Preheat oven to 375°.
Grease a 9-inch square baking pan.

Mix flour, oats, both sugars, baking powder and salt in a large bowl. Cut in butter with a pastry blender or two knives until crumbly. Reserve ¾ cup crumbly mixture; set aside. Press remaining mixture into prepared baking pan. Spread preserves evenly over crust; sprinkle with chocolate.

Mix reserved oat mixture and nuts in a bowl; sprinkle over chocolate; pat down lightly. Bake 30–35 minutes or until golden brown. Cool in pan until chocolate is firm. Cut into squares. Refrigerate leftovers.

Makes 25 squares.

GRANOLA STRAWBERRY SQUARES

Strawberry preserves in this sweet treat.

1½ cups granola cereal without raisins
¾ cup all-purpose flour
⅓ cup brown sugar, packed
½ teaspoon ground cinnamon
5 tablespoons cold butter

1 cup strawberry preserves

Preheat oven to 375°.
Generously grease a 9-inch square baking pan.

Mix granola, flour, sugar and cinnamon in a large bowl. Cut in butter until crumbly. Reserve a third of crumbly mixture for topping. Press remaining mixture into prepared pan. Bake 10 minutes. Remove from oven.

Spread preserves over warm crust. Sprinkle with reserved crumbly mixture. Return to oven; bake 15 minutes or until filling is bubbly around the edges. Cool on a wire rack. Cut into squares. Store in refrigerator.

Makes 16 squares.

DRIED STRAWBERRY AND
HAZELNUT BISCOTTI

Twice baked crunchy cookies…perfect for dunking!

½ cup butter, softened
¾ cup granulated sugar
2 eggs
2 teaspoons pure vanilla extract

1¾ cups all-purpose flour
½ teaspoon baking powder
½ teaspoon ground cinnamon

¼ teaspoon salt
¾ cup hazelnuts, toasted and coarsely chopped
½ cup coarsely chopped dried strawberries
1 teaspoon freshly grated orange zest

Preheat oven to 350°.

Beat butter in a large mixer bowl on high speed until fluffy. Beat in sugar until combined. Beat in eggs, one at a time, on low speed. Beat in vanilla extract.

Sift flour, baking powder, cinnamon and salt in a bowl; gradually stir into butter mixture just until blended. Stir in nuts, strawberries and zest. Place batter on a floured surface; divide in half. Place one half onto a greased baking sheet; shape into a log 12 inches long by 1½ inches round. Place log on one side of pan. Repeat with remaining batter, spacing at least 4 inches between logs.

Bake 25–30 minutes. Cool in pan on a wire rack 10 minutes. Cut log diagonally (in pan) with a serrated knife into ½-inch wide slices. Turn slices on their sides; return to oven and bake about 10 minutes and edges are golden. Use another ungreased baking sheet, if necessary, to hold more slices. Cool completely in pan on a wire rack.

Makes 4 dozen.

STRAWBERRY LINZER COOKIES

Ground almonds and strawberry in this sweet cookie.

1 cup butter, softened
¾ cup granulated sugar
2 eggs
½ teaspoon almond extract
2½ cups all-purpose flour
1 cup ground blanched slivered almonds

1 10-ounce jar strawberry all-fruit
    spread
½ cup sliced almonds

Beat butter and sugar in a large mixer bowl on medium speed until creamy.
Add eggs and almond extract, and continue beating until well mixed. Add
flour and ground almond; beat on low speed until well mixed.

Divide dough into eight equal parts. Roll each into an 8-inch log on a lightly
floured surface. Wrap logs into plastic food wrap; refrigerate until firm,
about 2 hours.

Preheat oven to 350°.
Place four logs each onto two large ungreased baking sheets. Pat each log
into a 2-inch wide strip. Press a 1-inch wide indentation lengthwise down
center of each strip using the back of a spoon.

Bake about 18 minutes or until edges are lightly browned. Remove from
oven. Spoon 2 tablespoonfuls strawberry spread into the indentation of
each log; sprinkle with sliced almonds. Cut diagonally into 1-inch pieces
while cookies are warm. Cool completely on baking sheets.

Makes 6 dozen.

STRAWBERRY THUMBPRINT COOKIES

Thumbprint cookies…always a favorite.

½ cup butter, room temperature
⅓ cup granulated sugar
1 large egg, separated
½ teaspoon pure vanilla extract
1 cup all-purpose flour
⅛ teaspoon salt

1 cup toasted almonds, pecans or walnuts, finely chopped
½ cup strawberry jam

Preheat oven to 350°.
Line a baking sheet with parchment paper.

Beat butter and sugar in a mixer bowl until light and fluffy. Add egg yolk
and vanilla extract; beat until combined. Mix flour and salt in a small bowl;
beat into butter mixture until combined.

Whisk egg white in a small bowl until frothy.
Place chopped nuts in another small bowl.

Roll dough into 1-inch balls. Dip balls, one at a time, into egg white and
then lightly roll into nuts. Place on prepared baking sheet. Make an indent
with thumb in center of each ball. Bake 9–11 minutes or until set and lightly
browned on the bottom. Remove from baking sheet; cool on wire rack.
Spoon jam in center of cookies.

Makes 1½ dozen.

33

STRAWBERRY WALNUT PINWHEEL COOKIES

Roll, cut and bake...a nice treat.

½ cup butter, softened
1 cup granulated sugar
1 egg
1 teaspoon pure vanilla extract
2 cups all-purpose flour
1 teaspoon baking powder

½ cup strawberry jam
1 cup chopped walnuts

Preheat oven to 375°.
Grease baking sheets.

Beat butter and sugar in a mixer bowl until creamy. Beat in egg and vanilla extract. Mix flour and baking powder in another bowl; gradually add to creamed mixture.

Roll dough out on a lightly floured surface into a 14x10-inch rectangle. Spread jam to within ½-inch of edges. Sprinkle evenly with walnuts. Roll dough, jelly-roll style, starting with a long side. Wrap in food plastic wrap and refrigerate 3 hours or more. Remove plastic wrap. Cut into ¼-inch slices. Place cookies 1 inch apart onto prepared baking sheets. Bake about 10–12 minutes or until lightly browned. Cool cookies on a wire rack.

Makes 4 dozen.

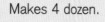

Beverages

FRESH STRAWBERRY LEMONADE

Fresh strawberries and fresh lemon juice…a perfect summer drink.

2 pints fresh strawberries, hulled
4 tablespoons superfine sugar

1 cup fresh lemon juice
1 cup superfine sugar

seltzer water
ice cubes

Puree strawberries with 4 tablespoons superfine sugar in a blender; pour mixture into a pitcher.
Add lemon juice and 1 cup superfine sugar. Stir until sugar is dissolved.
Pour over ice cubes in tall glasses. Add seltzer water. Serve.

Makes 4 servings.

FROSTY STRAWBERRY DAIQUIRI

Garnish with a fresh strawberry.

½ of 6-ounce can frozen lemonade concentrate
2 cups cold water
1 10-ounce package frozen strawberries in syrup
12 ice cubes
1 teaspoon granulated sugar
⅛ teaspoon rum extract

Process all ingredients in a blender on high speed until slushy. Pour into frosty glasses. Serve immediately.

Makes 3 servings.

KIKI'S STRAWBERRY DRINK

This frosty recipe is from my dear friend, from Blaine, Minnesota

1 cup strawberries, fresh or frozen
1 cup fresh orange juice
2 tablespoons granulated sugar
1 cup cracked ice

Place all ingredients in a blender; cover and process until strawberries are liquefied and ice is melted. Serve in frosted juice glasses.

Makes 2 servings.

NELAN'S STRAWBERRY SODA

Just two servings...one for a friend.

1 cup whole milk
½ cup fresh or frozen strawberries
½ cup vanilla ice cream, softened
2 tablespoons granulated sugar

1 cup ginger ale, chilled

Place milk, strawberries, vanilla ice cream and sugar in a blender. Cover and process until smooth. Pour into two tall glasses. Add ginger ale and serve immediately.

Makes 2 servings.

NON-ALCOHOLIC STRAWBERRY COLADA

Yes, you can double the recipe!

7 ripe fresh strawberries
5-ounces pineapple juice
1½-ounces coconut cream
1 cup crushed ice

Place all ingredients in a blender. Process at high speed until well blended. Pour mixture into a tall chilled glass. Garnish with a cherry and pineapple wedge. Serve immediately.

Makes 1 serving.

PINEAPPLE-STRAWBERRY PUNCH

A nice punch for bridal showers.

2 10-ounce packages frozen sweetened sliced strawberries, thawed
1 46-ounce can pineapple juice, chilled
4 cups lemon-lime soda, chilled

Puree strawberries in a food processor or blender. Pour into a large punch bowl. Stir in pineapple juice and chilled soda. Serve immediately. Refrigerate leftovers.

Makes about 3 quarts.

STRAWBERRY CHAMPAGNE PUNCH

Punch for a special occasion.

1 750-milliliter bottle champagne, chilled
2 liters ginger ale, chilled
2 10-ounce packages frozen strawberries, partially thawed

Place all ingredients in a large punch bowl. Stir gently; serve immediately. Refrigerate leftovers.

Makes 14 servings.

STRAWBERRY-LIME SLUSH

Try other juices for different flavored slush…so easy.

8 cups fresh strawberries
3 cups crushed ice
½ cup powdered sugar
¼ cup lime juice

Place 4 cups strawberries and ice in a blender or food processor. Cover and process on high until almost smooth, about 30 seconds. Pour mixture into a 2-quart pitcher.

Place remaining strawberries, powdered sugar and lime juice in blender or food processor. Cover and blend on high speed until almost smooth. Pour mixture into pitcher with first mixture; stir. Serve immediately.

Makes 4 servings.

STRAWBERRY MIXED BERRY SMOOTHIES

A delicious healthy smoothie.

2 cups frozen strawberries, partially thawed
2 cups frozen blueberries, partially thawed
2 cups frozen raspberries, partially thawed
1½ cups plain yogurt, chilled
½ cup cranberry juice, chilled
2 tablespoons honey or to taste

Working in batches, process all ingredients in a blender at high speed until smooth, about 3 minutes. Serve immediately in chilled tall glasses. Refrigerate leftovers.

Makes about 6 cups.

Breads
Muffins
Scones
Doughnuts

BANANA-STRAWBERRY QUICK BREAD

Cinnamon and walnuts in this quick bread.

1½ **cups all-purpose flour**
1 **teaspoon ground cinnamon**
¼ **teaspoon ground nutmeg**
½ **teaspoon baking soda**
½ **teaspoon salt**

2 **eggs**
1 **cup granulated sugar**
¼ **cup corn oil**
¾ **cup mashed fresh ripe strawberries**
½ **cup mashed ripe banana**
1 **teaspoon pure vanilla extract**
¾ **cup chopped walnuts**

Preheat oven to 350°.
Grease a 9x5-inch loaf pan.

Mix the first five ingredients in a medium size bowl.

Beat eggs, sugar and corn oil until smooth in another bowl. Stir in strawberries, banana and vanilla extract. Add to dry ingredients in medium bowl; stir until just moistened. Fold in walnuts. Pour batter into prepared pan. Bake 60–65 minutes or until a wooden pick inserted in center comes out clean. Cool in pan 10 minutes. Remove from pan; cool completely on a wire rack.

Makes 1 loaf.

PECAN STRAWBERRY BREAD

Share a loaf with your neighbor...with a cup of coffee of course.

2 cups granulated sugar
1¼ cups corn oil
4 eggs
1 teaspoon pure vanilla extract
1 16-ounce bag frozen strawberries, thawed and drained
    and mashed, or 1 pint fresh strawberries, finely diced

3 cups all-purpose flour
3 teaspoons ground cinnamon
1 teaspoon baking soda
1 teaspoon salt
1 cup chopped pecans

Preheat oven to 350°.
Grease bottoms only of two 9x5-inch baking pans.

Mix sugar and corn oil in a large bowl until blended. Stir in eggs and vanilla extract until blended. Stir in strawberries; mix well.

Mix flour, cinnamon, baking soda and salt in another bowl; stir into first mixture until just moistened. Stir in pecans. Pour batter into prepared pans.

Bake 60–70 minutes or until a wooden pick inserted in center comes out clean. Remove from oven; cool in pan 10 minutes. Loosen sides of bread from pans, then remove from pan. Cool completely on a wire rack before slicing. Refrigerate leftovers wrapped in food plastic wrap.

Makes 2 loaves.

RHUBARB-STRAWBERRY BREAD MACHINE LOAF

Rhubarb…not just for pies.

Ingredients for one 1½ pound loaf
½ **cup whole milk**
½ **cup water**
⅓ **cup chopped fresh rhubarb (2 ounces)**
⅓ **cup fresh sliced strawberries**
1 **teaspoon salt**
½ **teaspoon pure vanilla extract**
2 **tablespoons granulated sugar**
3 **cups unbleached all-purpose flour**
2 **teaspoons instant yeast**

Place all ingredients into the pan of your bread machine in the order recommended by the manufacturer. Set for white or basic bread, light setting, and press start. Check dough's consistency about 7 minutes after kneading cycle begins, adding additional water or flour to form a smooth, soft ball of dough. Allow the machine to complete its cycle. Remove the bread when it's done. Let cool completely on a wire rack before slicing.

Makes 1 loaf.

STRAWBERRY MACHINE BREAD

Spread strawberry jam on this good bread...buttered of course.

Ingredients for one 1½ pound loaf
¼ **cup water**
¼ **cup whipping cream**
1 cup sliced fresh strawberries
1 teaspoon salt
⅛ **teaspoon baking soda**
1 teaspoon pure vanilla extract
1 tablespoon granulated sugar
3½ **cups unbleached all-purpose flour**
2 teaspoons instant yeast

Place all ingredients into the pan of bread machine in the order recommended by the manufacturer. Set for white or basic bread, light setting, and press Start. Check the dough's consistency about 7 minutes after the kneading cycle begins, adding additional water or flour to form a smooth, soft ball of dough. Allow the machine to complete cycle. Remove the bread when it is done. Cool completely on a wire rack.

Makes 1 loaf.

WALNUT STRAWBERRY QUICK BREAD

For best slicing results, wrap loaf in food plastic wrap and let sit overnight...if you can wait!

½ cup chopped walnuts
1½ cups unbleached all-purpose flour
1 cup granulated sugar
½ teaspoon baking soda
¼ teaspoon salt
¼ teaspoon ground nutmeg

1 teaspoon lemon zest
½ teaspoon pure vanilla extract
2 eggs
1¼ cups mashed ripe hulled strawberries
⅓ cup corn oil

Preheat oven to 350°.
Grease and flour a 9x5-inch loaf pan.

Mix first six ingredients in a medium size mixing bowl.

Whisk remaining ingredients in another bowl until blended; add mixture into dry mixture and whisk until well blended. Pour batter into prepared pan. Bake 55–60 minutes or until a wooden pick inserted in center comes out clean. Cool in pan 15 minutes. Remove from pan; cool completely on a wire rack.

Makes 1 loaf.

BANANA-STRAWBERRY MUFFINS

Stir up a batch of these delicious muffins for a special time.

⅔ cup granulated sugar
½ cup corn oil
2 eggs
⅔ cup mashed ripe bananas
1 teaspoon pure vanilla extract

1⅔ cups all-purpose flour
1 teaspoon baking soda
½ teaspoon salt
¾ cup finely chopped fresh strawberries

Preheat oven to 375°.
Line a 12 cup muffin pan with paper baking cups.

Mix sugar, oil and eggs in a medium bowl until well blended. Stir in bananas and vanilla extract.

Mix flour, baking soda and salt in a small bowl; stir into sugar mixture until just combined, do not over mix. Stir in strawberries. Spoon batter evenly into prepared muffin cups. Bake 17–21 minutes or until a wooden pick inserted in center comes out clean. Remove from pan. Serve warm or cool on a wire rack. Refrigerate leftovers.

Makes 12 muffins.

FRESH STRAWBERRY MUFFINS

For added goodness, sprinkle ¼ teaspoon granulated sugar on top of each muffin before baking. Serve warm with softened butter and jam.

2½ cups all-purpose flour
½ cup granulated sugar
1 teaspoon baking soda
½ teaspoon salt

1½ cups buttermilk
⅓ cup melted butter
2 eggs, beaten
1 teaspoon pure vanilla extract
1 pint fresh strawberries, hulled and chopped

Preheat oven to 400°.
Paper-line or grease muffin pan.

Mix flour, sugar, baking soda and salt in a large bowl.

Whisk buttermilk, butter, egg and vanilla extract in another bowl; stir in to dry mixture just until moistened. Stir in strawberries. Spoon batter evenly into prepared muffin cups. Bake 20–25 minutes. Remove muffins from pan. Serve warm or cool on a wire rack. Refrigerate leftovers.

Makes 12 muffins.

OAT BRAN STRAWBERRY MUFFINS

A cholesterol-free muffin recipe, adapted from my book, *The Muffins Are Coming*.

Dry ingredients
¾ cup oat bran
1½ cups all-purpose flour
½ cup granulated sugar
2 teaspoons baking powder
½ teaspoon salt
1 tablespoon non-fat dry milk

Wet ingredients
⅔ cup skim milk
3 egg whites, beaten with 1 teaspoon corn oil
¼ cup margarine, melted and slightly cooled
1 teaspoon pure vanilla extract
1 teaspoon fresh lemon juice
2 cups fresh firm strawberries cut into small pieces

Preheat oven to 400°.
Grease or paper-line muffin pan.

Mix all dry ingredients in a large bowl until well blended.

Mix all wet ingredients in a medium bowl until blended; add to dry ingredients. Stir only to moisten, but batter is lumpy. Spoon batter evenly into prepared muffin pan. Bake 20–25 minutes. Remove from pan to a wire rack. Refrigerate leftovers.

Makes 12 muffins.

PEANUT BUTTER N' STRAWBERRY JELLY MUFFINS

The kids will love these…big kids too.

2 cups all-purpose flour
2 teaspoons baking powder
¾ teaspoon baking soda
¼ teaspoon salt

2 eggs, beaten
¾ cup apple juice concentrate

½ cup chunky peanut butter
¼ cup whole milk
1 teaspoon pure vanilla extract
3 tablespoons butter, melted and
slightly cooled
⅓ cup 100% strawberry spreadable
fruit

Preheat oven to 350°.
Spray muffin tin with nonstick cooking spray.

Mix flour, baking powder, baking soda and salt in a large bowl.

Mix eggs, apple juice concentrate, peanut butter, milk, vanilla extract and butter in another bowl. Add to dry mixture and stir only to moisten.

Spoon half the batter evenly into prepared cups. Spoon 1¼ teaspoons spreadable fruit into the center of each, then top evenly with remaining batter. Bake 20–25 minutes or until a wooden pick inserted one inch from edge comes out clean. Cool 5 minutes in pan. Remove from pan to a wire rack; cool completely. Refrigerate leftovers.

Makes 12 muffins.

COCONUT STRAWBERRY SCONES WITH CITRUS BUTTER

Dried strawberries are not easy to find yet, but can be found in gourmet shops and on the internet.

Citrus Butter
- **½ cup butter, softened**
- **1 tablespoon powdered sugar**
- **1 teaspoon freshly grated lemon peel**
- **1 teaspoon freshly grated orange peel**

Scones
- **2 cups all-purpose flour**
- **¼ cup granulated sugar**
- **¼ teaspoon salt**
- **½ cup cold butter**
- **1 egg, beaten**
- **½ cup light cream (half & half)**
- **⅓ cup sweetened flaked coconut**
- **½ cup dried strawberries, chopped**
- **1 teaspoon freshly grated lemon peel**
- **1 tablespoon coarse grain sugar**

Citrus Butter: Beat ingredients in a bowl until smooth. Refrigerate.

Preheat oven to 375°. Grease a baking sheet.

Scones: Mix flour, ¼ cup sugar, baking powder and salt in a medium bowl; cut in butter with a pastry blender until mixture resembles coarse crumbs. Mix remaining scones ingredients in a small bowl. Add to flour mixture and stir just until flour mixture is moistened.

Knead dough lightly 8–10 times on a lightly floured surface. Pat dough into a 7-inch circle. Place onto prepared baking sheet. Cut into 8 wedges but do not separate wedges. Sprinkle with coarse sugar. Bake 20–25 minutes or until golden brown. Cool 15 minutes. Cut wedges apart; remove from baking sheet. Serve warm with citrus butter.

Makes 8 scones.

ORANGE-STRAWBERRY SCONES

Great treat for tea...serve warm with butter and strawberry jam.

2 cups all-purpose flour
¼ cup granulated sugar
3 tablespoons baking powder
½ teaspoon salt
½ cup butter, cut into small pieces
½ cup chopped dried strawberries

1 egg
½ cup heavy cream
zest of 1 medium size fresh orange

Preheat oven to 350°.
Lightly grease a scone pan.

Pulse flour, sugar, baking powder and salt in a food processor until combined. Add butter; pulse to form pea size crumbs. Place mixture into a large bowl. Stir in strawberries just until combined.

Whisk egg, cream and zest in a small bowl until blended; add to flour mixture. Stir with a fork to form moist dough, do not over mix. Place dough on a lightly floured surface; press dough with hands to form a ball. Roll out, using more flour if needed, into a 10-inch round about ¾-inch thick. Cut dough into 8 equal wedges. Press wedges into prepared pan. Bake about 25 minutes or until golden. Invert pan on a wire rack to remove scones. Cool 10 minutes. Refrigerate leftovers.

Makes 8 scones.

STRAWBERRY JELLY DOUGHNUTS

Strawberry jam is used in these "jelly" doughnuts!

¾ cup whole milk
¼ cup butter or margarine
¼ cup granulated sugar
½ teaspoon salt
½ teaspoon pure vanilla extract
1 teaspoon finely grated fresh lemon zest
1 package dry yeast dissolved in ¼ cup warm water

2 large eggs
3½ to 4 cups all-purpose flour
⅔ cup strawberry jam
vegetable oil for deep-frying

Mix milk, butter, sugar and salt in a wide saucepan; stir over medium heat until butter is melted. Pour mixture into a large mixing bowl. Stir in vanilla extract and lemon zest. Set aside to cool. When barely warm to touch, stir in dissolved yeast mixture.

Separate 1 egg and reserve egg white. Beat the yolk and other whole egg in a bowl; add to milk mixture. Beat in 3 cups flour with a wooden spoon until moist, stiff dough is formed. Knead dough on a lightly floured surface kneading enough of remaining flour to form a soft, but not sticky dough. Place dough in a greased bowl; cover and let rise until doubled in bulk. Punch dough down; roll out to ¼-inch thickness. Cut dough with a 3-inch biscuit cutter. Spoon a generous dollop jam onto center of half the rounds. Whisk egg white in a bowl until foamy, then brush dough surrounding jam lightly with egg white. Top with remaining rounds and press to seal. Place on a baking sheet; cover and let rest 10 minutes.

Heat about 3-inches deep oil in deep heavy pot to 370°. Place doughnuts with a slotted spoon in hot oil; fry 2 at a time, turning occasionally until puffed and golden brown, about 3–4 minutes. Remove with slotted spoon; drain on paper towels. Dust with powdered sugar.

Makes 2 dozen.

Cakes

ANGEL FOOD STRAWBERRY TUNNEL CREAM CAKE

A beautiful cake...creamy and delicious.

1 10-inch prepared angel food cake

2 3-ounce packages cream cheese, softened
1 14-ounce can sweetened condensed milk
⅓ cup fresh lemon juice
1 teaspoon almond extract
2 drops red food coloring, optional

1 cup chopped fresh strawberries
1 12-ounce container frozen non-dairy whipped topping, thawed, divided
fresh strawberry for garnish

Place cake on a serving plate. Cut 1-inch slice crosswise from top of cake with a serrated knife; set aside.

With a sharp knife, cut around cake 1-inch from center hole and 1-inch from outer edge, leaving cake walls 1-inch thick. Remove cake from center, leaving 1-inch base on bottom of cake. Tear cake removed from center into bite-size pieces and reserve.

Beat cream cheese in a large mixer bowl on medium speed until fluffy. Gradually beat in sweetened condensed milk until smooth. Beat in almond extract and food coloring. Stir in strawberries. Fold in 1 cup whipped topping; fill cavity of cake with mixture.

Replace top slice of cake, and frost with remaining whipped topping. Immediately refrigerate; chill until set, about 3 hours. Garnish with fresh strawberries. Store in refrigerator.

Makes one 10-inch angel food cake; 10 servings.

CHOCOLATE SPONGE CAKE WITH STRAWBERRIES AND KIWI

Use other fresh fruit along with strawberries if desired.

Cake
1 cup powdered sugar
4 eggs, room temperature
1 tablespoon crème de cacao
 or 1 teaspoon pure vanilla extract
½ cup all-purpose flour
¼ cup Dutch process
 unsweetened cocoa
⅛ teaspoon salt

2 tablespoons butter, melted

Topping
3 cups fresh ripe strawberries,
 halved
1 kiwi fruit, peeled and thinly sliced
 and halved
1 10-ounce jar apple jelly, melted

Preheat oven to 375°.
Grease and flour 10-inch tart pan with removable bottom. Place pan on baking sheet.

Cake: Beat powdered sugar, eggs and crème de cacao in a large bowl on high speed until thick and mixture is double in volume, about 8 minutes. Mixture should be the consistency of soft whipped cream.

Mix flour, cocoa and salt in a small bowl; gently stir mixture into egg mixture by hand a little at a time, just until flour mixture disappears. Gently stir in melted butter. Spoon batter into prepared pan. Bake 20–24 minutes or until a wooden pick inserted in center comes out clean. Remove from oven; cool completely. Remove from pan.

Topping: Place strawberries and kiwi fruit decoratively on top of cake when serving. Drizzle with melted jelly. Refrigerate leftovers.

Makes 12 servings.

CHOCOLATE STRAWBERRY ICEBOX CAKE

A slice of this delicious cake will long be remembered.

1½ pints fresh strawberries, divided
1½ cups heavy whipping cream
3 tablespoons powdered sugar
1 teaspoon pure vanilla extract
2 tablespoons strawberry preserves

35 chocolate wafer cookies
(about 9-ounce package)

hull and thinly slice 1 pint
strawberries, set aside
remaining ½ pint.

Beat cream, sugar and vanilla extract in a large bowl with a mixer on medium speed to stiff peaks. Remove 2 cups whipped cream; place in another bowl, cover and refrigerate. Gently fold sliced strawberries and preserves with a rubber spatula into remaining whipped cream in bowl.

Spread about 1 heaping tablespoon strawberry cream mixture on one side of each 6 cookies. Stack cookies on top of one another. Top the stack with a plain cookie.

Repeat stacking cookies with strawberry cream mixture until all cookies and cream are used, making 5 stacks of 7 cookies each.

Turn each stack on its side. Place stacks, one behind the other, with rounded edges touching, to form a log on a platter. Frost log with reserved whipped cream; cover and refrigerate cake at least 6 hours, allowing cookies to soften. To serve, hull reserved strawberries; cut into quarters and place all around edge of log on platter. Refrigerate leftovers.

Makes 10 servings.

COCONUT STRAWBERRY CAKE

A cake mix makes this easy to prepare. When serving, top with sweetened sliced fresh strawberries and a dollop of sweetened whipped cream.

1 18.25-ounce package white or yellow cake mix
1¼ cups shredded coconut
1 8-ounce package cream cheese, softened
1¼ cups powdered sugar
1 cup fresh ripe strawberries, mashed
1 teaspoon pure vanilla extract

Preheat oven to 350°.
Grease and flour a 13x9-inch baking pan.

Prepare cake mix following package directions.

Spread coconut onto bottom of prepared pan. Pour half of the cake batter over coconut.

Beat cream cheese until fluffy in a mixer bowl. Beat in sugar until smooth. Beat in mashed strawberries and vanilla extract. Drop large dollops of mixture over cake batter. Pour remaining batter over top. Bake 30–35 minutes. Cool slightly, then refrigerate overnight before serving.

Makes 12 Servings.

CREAM CHEESE-FROSTED COCONUT STRAWBERRY CAKE

A cake mix makes it easy…strawberries, coconut, pecans and cream cheese makes it delicious.

Cake
1 18.25-ounce plain white cake mix
1 3-ounce package strawberry flavor gelatin mix, dry
1½ cups fresh ripe strawberries, thoroughly mashed
1 cup corn oil
½ cup whole milk
4 large eggs
1 teaspoon pure vanilla extract

1 cup frozen unsweetened grated coconut, thawed
½ cup chopped pecans

Frosting
1 8-ounce package cream cheese, softened
½ cup butter (1 stick), room temperature
3½ cups powdered sugar
¾ cup fresh ripe strawberries, mashed to make ½ cup, then well drained
½ cup frozen unsweetened grated coconut, thawed
½ cup chopped pecans

Preheat oven to 350°.
Grease three 9-inch round cake pans with solid shortening; dust with flour.

Cake: Beat first seven ingredients in a mixer bowl on low speed 1 minute. Beat on medium speed 2 minutes. Fold in 1 cup coconut and ½ cup pecans. Divide batter into prepared pans. Bake until cake just starts to pull away from sides of pan, about 28–30 minutes. Cool in pan 10 minutes on a wire rack. Remove from pans; cool completely on a wire rack.

Frosting: Beat cream cheese and butter in a mixer bowl on medium speed until fluffy. Add powdered sugar and drained strawberries; beat on medium speed until well blended. Fold in ½ cup coconut and ½ cup pecans. Spread frosting between layers, top, and sides of cake. Refrigerate 20 minutes. Serve, or cover and store in refrigerator up to one week.

Makes 10 servings.

DORIE'S DOUBLE STRAWBERRY POKE CAKE

Strawberry cake mix and strawberry topping…double good!

1 18.25-ounce package strawberry cake mix

1 14-ounce can sweetened condensed milk
1 pint frozen sliced strawberries, thawed
1 12-ounce container frozen nondairy whipped topping, thawed

Prepare and bake cake mix as directed on package for a 13x9x2-inch baking pan. Remove from oven and cool to room temperature. Poke holes all over cake with the handle of a wooden spoon.

Gradually pour sweetened condensed milk over cake, making sure it seeps through the holes. Fold strawberries into whipped topping in a bowl. Spread mixture over cake. Refrigerate and chill. Store in refrigerator.

Makes 12 servings.

LAYERED STRAWBERRY CAKE

A cake mix is used for this delicious strawberry and cream cake.

1 18.25-ounce package butter recipe yellow cake mix
⅔ cup buttermilk
½ cup butter or margarine, softened
3 large eggs
1 teaspoon pure vanilla extract

½ cup strawberry preserves, divided
2 cups whipping cream
3 tablespoons powdered sugar
2 quarts fresh strawberries, sliced

Preheat oven to 350°.
Grease and flour two 9-inch round cake pans.

Beat cake mix, buttermilk, butter, eggs and vanilla extract in a large mixer bowl on low speed until moistened. Beat on medium speed 4 minutes. Pour batter into prepared pans. Bake 18–20 minutes or until a wooden pick inserted in center comes out clean. Cool in pan on a wire rack 10 minutes; remove from pans. Brush top of each layer with 2 tablespoons preserves. Cool completely on a wire rack.

Beat remaining preserves with whipping cream and powdered sugar in a bowl on high speed until stiff peaks form. Place 1 cake layer on a serving plate. Top with half of sliced strawberries, then top with half of whipped cream mixture. Repeat: cake layer, strawberries and whipped cream mixture. Serve or refrigerate. Refrigerate leftovers.

Makes 12 servings.

MOLTEN CHOCOLATE CAKES WITH STRAWBERRY FOOL

Molten chocolate oozing and strawberries in cream...delightful.

4 tablespoons unsalted butter,
 room temperature
⅓ cup granulated sugar
3 large eggs

⅓ cup all-purpose flour
¼ teaspoon salt
8 ounces bittersweet chocolate,
 melted and slightly cooled (do not use semi-sweet chocolate)

Strawberry Fool
1 cup fresh strawberries, halved,
 pureed with 2 tablespoons
 granulated sugar
1 cup whipping cream, whipped
 with ¼ cup granulated sugar and
 1 teaspoon pure vanilla extract

Preheat oven to 400°.

Generously butter 4 cups of a standard muffin-baking pan. Sprinkle each with granulated sugar; tap to remove excess.

Cakes: Beat butter and ⅓ cup granulated sugar in a mixer bowl with an electric mixer until fluffy. Beat in eggs, one at a time. Beat in flour, and salt on low speed just until mixed, scraping down sides as needed. Fold in chocolate. Divide batter equally into prepared pan. Bake just until tops are set, about 8–10 minutes. Remove from oven; let cool in pan 10 minutes.

Strawberry Fool: Gently stir pureed strawberries into whipped cream.

To serve, turn out cakes onto a dessert plate. Serve with a dollop of strawberry fool. Refrigerate leftovers.

Makes 4 servings.

PINEAPPLE-STRAWBERRY GELATIN CAKE

A cake mix is used in this fruit and marshmallow filled cake. Top with thawed strawberry whipped topping when serving.

2 cups chopped fresh strawberries
1 20-ounce can crushed pineapple, drained
1 8-serving size package strawberry flavor gelatin mix
3 cups miniature marshmallows

1 18.25-ounce package white cake mix
2 eggs

Preheat oven to 350°.
Grease a 13x9x2-inch baking pan.

Spread strawberries evenly onto bottom of prepared pan. Top evenly with drained pineapple. Sprinkle with dry gelatin mix. Top with marshmallows.

Prepare cake batter as directed on package, omitting oil and using the 2 eggs and water as directed. Pour batter evenly over marshmallows.

Bake 50 to 55 minutes or until a wooden pick inserted in center comes out clean. Cool 15 minutes before serving. Refrigerate leftovers.

Makes 16 servings.

RUTH'S CHOCOLATE EARTHQUAKE CAKE WITH STRAWBERRIES

Top each serving of this delicious earthquake cake with small fresh strawberries (hot lava rocks) and whipped topping (spewed ashes)!

1 cup chopped pecans
1 can sweetened flaked
   coconut (3.5-ounce)

1 18-ounce package German
   chocolate cake mix

1 8-ounce package cream cheese,
   softened
1/2 cup butter, melted and cooled
1 16-ounce box powdered sugar
1/2 teaspoon pure vanilla extract

fresh strawberries
whipped topping

Preheat oven to 350°.
Grease and flour a 13x9-inch baking pan.

Sprinkle pecans and coconut to cover bottom of prepared baking pan.

Prepare cake mix according to package directions. Pour prepared batter over pecan and coconut layer.

Mix cream cheese, butter, sugar and vanilla extract in a medium bowl until well blended. Drop dollops of mixture by the teaspoonfuls on top of batter.

Bake 40–42 minutes (you will not be able to test with a toothpick for doneness, as the cake will appear sticky even when done). Do not over bake. The icing sinks into the batter as it bakes, forming a white ribbon inside (earthquake crack), thus the name earthquake. Refrigerate leftovers.

Makes 12 servings.

STRAWBERRY POUND CAKE WITH STRAWBERRY SAUCE

Double strawberry delight…serve with whipped cream, of course.

Cake

1 16-ounce package frozen sweetened sliced strawberries, thawed, drained and reserving ½ cup juice; set aside.
1 cup butter-flavored shortening
2 cups granulated sugar
4 eggs
3 cups all-purpose flour
1 teaspoon baking soda
½ teaspoon baking powder
½ teaspoon salt
⅔ cup buttermilk
½ cup chopped pecans
1 teaspoon pure vanilla extract
¼ teaspoon strawberry extract

Sauce

1 cup granulated sugar
½ cup sliced fresh strawberries
½ teaspoon pure vanilla extract
¼ teaspoon strawberry extract

Preheat oven to 325°.
Grease and flour 10-inch fluted tube pan.

Cake: Beat shortening and 2 cups sugar in a mixer bowl on medium speed until creamy. Beat in eggs one at a time. Mix flour, baking soda, baking powder and salt in a medium bowl; beat into creamed mixture alternately with buttermilk. Stir in pecans and chopped strawberries, 1 teaspoon vanilla and ¼ teaspoon strawberry extract. Pour batter into prepared pan. Bake about 1 hour and 25 minutes or until a wooden pick inserted near center comes out clean. Cool 10 minutes. Remove from pan to a wire rack.

Sauce: Stir 1 cup sugar and reserved juice in a small saucepan. Add fresh strawberries. Bring to a boil; cook and stir one minute. Stir in ½ teaspoon vanilla and ¼ teaspoon strawberry extract. Brush warm cake with a little sauce. Serve cake with remaining sauce. Refrigerate leftovers.

Makes 12 servings.

STRAWBERRY-TOPPED SOUR CREAM SNACK CAKE

Homemade white cake topped with strawberries and whipped cream.

Cake
⅓ cup butter, softened
1 cup granulated sugar
3 egg whites
¼ cup dairy sour cream
1 teaspoon pure vanilla extract
1½ cups all-purpose flour
2 teaspoons baking powder

¼ teaspoon salt
⅓ cup whole milk

Topping
1 10-ounce package frozen sliced
   sweetened strawberries, thawed
1 tablespoon cornstarch
sweetened whipped cream

Preheat oven to 350°.
Grease and flour an 8-inch square baking pan.

Cake: Beat butter and sugar in a large bowl on medium speed until creamy. Beat in egg whites until light and fluffy. Stir in sour cream and vanilla extract. Reduce speed to low; add flour, baking powder, salt and milk. Beat until just combined. Spread batter into prepared pan.

Bake 30–35 minutes or until a wooden pick inserted in center comes out clean. Cool completely.

Topping: Cook and stir strawberries and cornstarch in a medium saucepan over medium heat until mixture boils and thickens. Cool 15 minutes. Spread evenly over cake. Cover and refrigerate until chilled. Top with whipped cream when serving. Refrigerate leftovers.

Makes 9 servings.

SANDRA'S STRAWBERRY CAKE

This moist strawberry cake is sure to become one of your favorites.

Cake
1 18.25-ounce package yellow cake mix

1 6-ounce box strawberry flavor gelatin mix
2 cups boiling water
1½ cups cold water

Topping
1 10-ounce package frozen strawberries, thawed
1 8-ounce container frozen nondairy whipped topping

Cake: Prepare and bake cake following package directions using a 13x9-inch baking pan. Remove from oven; cool in pan. Punch holes all over top of cooled cake with toothpick.

Mix strawberry gelatin mix with boiling water in a bowl, stirring until completely dissolved. Stir in cold water. Reserve ½ cup mixture for topping. Slowly pour remaining mixture over cake, saturating cake evenly all over.

Topping: Place ½ cup reserved gelatin mixture and thawed strawberries in a blender and process until pureed. Pour mixture over whipped topping in a large bowl. Mix until blended. Spread mixture over cake. Refrigerate immediately and chill at least 4–6 hours. Store in the refrigerator.

Makes 12 servings.

Cheesecakes

BANANA FUDGE CHEESECAKE WITH STRAWBERRIES

Top with sweetened whipped cream when serving.

Crust
2 cups graham cracker crumbs
2 tablespoons granulated sugar
¼ cup butter, melted

Topping
2 cups fresh ripe strawberries,
halved
chocolate fudge ice cream
topping, heated

Filling
2 8-ounce packages cream
cheese, softened
¾ cup granulated sugar
1½ teaspoons pure vanilla extract
3 eggs
½ cup dairy sour cream
⅓ cup semi-sweet chocolate
chips, melted
2 very ripe bananas, mashed

Preheat oven to 425°.
Line bottom of a 12-inch springform pan with cooking foil, butter lightly; butter rim, then attach to bottom of pan.

Crust: Mix crust ingredients in a bowl; pack into bottom of prepared pan.

Filling: Beat cream cheese and sugar in a mixer bowl on medium speed until smooth and fluffy. Add vanilla. Beat in eggs, one at a time. Beat in sour cream. Remove one third of creamed mixture to a small bowl and stir in melted chocolate.

Add mashed bananas to non-chocolate mixture. Pour two thirds of non-chocolate mixture into crust. Top with chocolate mixture, then with remaining non-chocolate mixture. Bake 15 minutes. Reduce heat to 225°. Bake about 1 hour or until center is almost set. Chill uncovered. Arrange strawberries on top of cheesecake. Drizzle with fudge ice cream topping. Refrigerate leftovers.

Makes 16 servings.

73

CHOCOLATE CHIP CHEESECAKE WITH STRAWBERRY SAUCE

Chocolate and strawberries…always a treat.

Crust
2 cups chocolate creme sandwich cookie crumbs
6 tablespoons butter, melted

Filling
3 8-ounce packages cream cheese, softened

¾ cup powdered sugar
3 large eggs
⅓ cup whipping cream
1 tablespoon pure vanilla extract
1½ cups semi-sweet chocolate chips

Crust: Mix crust ingredients in a bowl until blended. Press mixture into bottom and 1-inch up sides of a lightly buttered 10-inch springform pan. Freeze 15 minutes while preparing filling.

Preheat oven to 325°.

Filling: Beat cream cheese and sugar in a mixer bowl on medium high speed 3 minutes. Reduce speed to low. Beat in eggs, one at a time. Beat in whipping cream and vanilla extract on medium-high speed 3 minutes. Pour ¾ of batter into prepared crust. Sprinkle chocolate chips over batter, then pour remaining batter over chips. Bake 1 hour and 15 minutes. Turn oven off and leave cheesecake in oven with door closed for 1½ hours. Refrigerate 8 hours before serving. When serving, top with strawberry sauce. Refrigerate leftovers.

Sauce: 2 cups fresh or frozen strawberries, thawed, pureed in a blender with 2 tablespoons granulated sugar; refrigerate until serving.

Makes 14 servings.

CHOCOLATE STRAWBERRY CHEESECAKE

A fudge cake mix is used to make this delicious dessert.

1 18-ounce package moist chocolate fudge cake mix
½ cup butter, softened

2 8-ounce packages cream cheese, softened
1 6-ounce container strawberry yogurt
1 16-ounce tub ready to spread rich and creamy chocolate frosting

½ teaspoon pure vanilla extract
3 eggs

1½ cups sliced fresh strawberries
½ cup fresh raspberries
1 21-ounce can strawberry pie filling, slightly chilled
whipped cream

Preheat oven to 325°.
Grease bottom of a 13x9x2-inch baking pan with solid shortening.

Beat cake mix and butter in a large bowl with an electric mixer on low speed until crumbly. Remove 1 cup mixture; set aside. Press remaining crumbly mixture in bottom of prepared pan.

Beat cream cheese in a large bowl on medium speed until fluffy. Add yogurt, frosting and vanilla extract; beat until smooth. Beat in eggs one at a time. Pour mixture into prepared pan. Sprinkle top evenly with reserved crumbly mixture. Bake until center is set and dry to touch, about 45 minutes. Remove from oven; refrigerate and chill. Refrigerate leftovers.

Mix berries and pie filling in a bowl just before serving. Top each serving as desired. Top with a dollop of whipped cream. Refrigerate leftovers.

Makes 14 servings.

CHOCOLATE TRUFFLE CHEESECAKE WITH STRAWBERRIES

Enjoy a slice of this chocolate crusted chocolate cheesecake.

Crust
1 cup chocolate wafer crumbs
3 tablespoons butter or
  margarine, melted

Sauce
1 10-ounce package strawberries
  in syrup, thawed
3 tablespoons whipping cream

Filling
2 8-ounce packages cream
  cheese, softened
⅔ cup granulated sugar
2 eggs
1 cup real semi-sweet chocolate
  chips, melted
½ teaspoon pure vanilla extract

Preheat oven to 350°.
Lightly butter a 9-inch springform pan.

Crust: Mix all crust ingredients in a small bowl; press onto bottom of prepared pan. Bake 10 minutes.

Filling: Beat cream cheese and sugar in a large mixer bowl on medium speed until well blended. Beat in eggs, one at a time. Blend in chocolate and vanilla extract. Pour mixture over crust. Bake 45 minutes. Loosen cake from side of pan; cool before removing side of pan. Refrigerate and chill. When serving, spoon strawberry sauce onto each serving plate. Place a slice of cheesecake over sauce. Refrigerate leftovers.

Sauce: Process strawberries in a food processor until smooth. Strain. Stir in cream. Refrigerate leftovers.

Makes 10 servings.

FROZEN MOCHA CHEESECAKE WITH STRAWBERRY TOPPING

A favorite frozen dessert with my family.

1½ cups creme-filled chocolate
   sandwich cookie crumbs
¼ cup whole almonds, toasted
   and chopped
¼ cup granulated sugar
¼ cup butter, melted

Topping
2 tablespoons light corn syrup
1 10-ounce package frozen sliced
   strawberries, pureed to equal ½ cup
1 cup whipping cream, stiffly
   whipped with 2 tablespoons sugar
¼ cup each, toasted chopped almonds
   and reserved cookie crumb mixture

Filling
1 8-ounce package cream
   cheese, softened
1 14-ounce can sweetened
   condensed milk
⅔ cup chocolate syrup listed
   below or use purchased
   chocolate syrup
1½ tablespoons instant coffee
   granules, dissolved in
   1 tablespoon hot water
1 teaspoon pure vanilla extract
1 cup whipping cream, whipped

Crust: Mix all crust ingredients in a bowl; reserve ¼ cup. Press remaining mixture onto bottom of a buttered 9-inch springform pan. Chill.

Filling: Beat cream cheese in a large mixer bowl until fluffy. Gradually beat in sweetened condensed milk, chocolate syrup, coffee mixture and vanilla extract until smooth. Fold in whipped cream. Pour mixture into prepared crust. Freeze 6 hours or until firm.

Topping: In a bowl, fold corn syrup and strawberry puree in whipped cream. Spoon on top of frozen cheesecake when serving. Sprinkle outer edge with almonds and reserved crumb mixture. Freeze leftovers.

Syrup (optional): Stir 6 tablespoons cocoa powder, ¾ cup granulated sugar, pinch salt, and ½ cup hot water until smooth in a small saucepan. Bring to a boil over medium heat. Cook and stir constantly 3 minutes. Remove from heat stir in 1 teaspoon pure vanilla extract. Refrigerate. Makes 1 cup.

Makes 10 servings.

HANNAH'S STRAWBERRY CHEESECAKE

This is my mother-in-law's recipe...one of my favorites.

Crust
1¼ cups graham cracker crumbs
¼ cup granulated sugar
¼ cup butter, melted

Filling
1 8-ounce package cream
   cheese, softened
½ cup granulated sugar
2 eggs, well beaten
½ cup dairy sour cream

1 teaspoon pure vanilla extract

Topping
2 10-ounce packages sweetened
   frozen strawberries, thawed,
   drained and juice reserved
1½ tablespoons cornstarch
1 teaspoon fresh lemon juice
½ teaspoon pure vanilla extract
sweetened whipped cream

Preheat oven to 350°.

Crust: Mix all crust ingredients in a bowl. Press mixture onto bottom and a little up sides of an 8-inch square-baking pan.

Filling: Beat all filling ingredients in a mixer bowl with an electric mixer until creamy. Pour mixture into prepared crust. Bake 20 to 28 minutes or until set. Remove from oven. Cool in pan on a wire rack.

Topping: Stir reserved strawberry juice and cornstarch in a saucepan until blended; cook and stir over medium heat until thickened. Stir in thawed strawberries and lemon juice; cook 1 minute. Stir in vanilla. Remove from heat. Cool completely. Spread mixture over cooled cheesecake and immediately refrigerate. Chill well before serving. Cut into squares. Garnish with sweetened whipped cream as desired when serving. Refrigerate leftovers.

Makes 8 servings.

KEY LIME CHEESECAKE WITH FRESH STRAWBERRY SAUCE

If key limes are not available, use regular limes.

Crust
2 cups graham cracker crumbs
¼ cup granulated sugar
½ cup butter, melted

Filling
3 8-ounce packages cream cheese, softened

1¼ cups granulated sugar
3 large eggs
1 8-ounce container dairy sour cream
1½ teaspoons freshly grated key lime rind
½ cup fresh key lime juice
1 teaspoon pure vanilla extract

Sauce
1¼ cups fresh strawberries, process in food processor until smooth with ¼ cup granulated sugar and 1 teaspoon freshly grated key lime rind

Preheat oven to 350°.

Crust: Mix all crust ingredients in a bowl; press mixture onto bottom and 1-inch up sides of a greased 9-inch springform pan. Bake 8 minutes. Cool.

Reduce heat to 325°.
Filling: Beat cream cheese in a large bowl on medium speed until fluffy. Gradually beat in 1¼ cups sugar until blended. Beat in eggs, one at a time. Stir in sour cream, lime rind, lime juice and vanilla extract. Pour mixture into prepared crust. Bake 1 hour and 10 minutes. Turn oven off. Let stand in over with door partially opened 15 minutes. Remove from oven. Run a thin knife around edge of pan, releasing sides. Cool completely in pan. Immediately cover and refrigerate; chill 8 hours. Top with strawberry sauce when serving. Refrigerate leftovers.

Makes 10 servings.

NEW YORK STYLE
STRAWBERRY-SWIRLED CHEESECAKE

There are many versions of New York style cheesecake. This is one of them. Top with sweetened whipped cream and fresh strawberries.

Crust
1 cup graham cracker crumbs
3 tablespoons granulated sugar
3 tablespoons butter, melted

Filling
4 8-ounce packages cream cheese, softened

1 cup granulated sugar
1 tablespoon pure vanilla extract
1 cup dairy sour cream
4 eggs
1 16-ounce package frozen sweetened strawberries, thawed and drained and pureed

Preheat oven to 325°.
Line a 13x9x2-inch baking pan with foil; ends extending over sides of pan.

Crust: Mix all crust ingredients in a bowl. Press firmly onto bottom of prepared pan. Bake 10 minutes.

Filling: Beat cream cheese, sugar and vanilla extract in a large bowl on medium speed until well blended. Beat in sour cream. Beat in eggs, one at a time just until blended. Pour batter into prepared crust. Add strawberry puree and swirl with a knife. Bake about 45 minutes or until center is almost set. Cool completely. Refrigerate at least 4 hours before serving. Lift from pan using foil handles. Refrigerate leftovers.

Makes 16 servings.

PINEAPPLE COCONUT CHEESECAKE WITH STRAWBERRY SAUCE

A good choice for entertaining…make ahead except for sauce.

Crust
1⅓ cups graham cracker crumbs
¼ cup butter, melted
2 tablespoons granulated sugar

Filling
4 8-ounce package cream cheese, softened
1 cup granulated sugar
4 eggs
1 cup dairy sour cream

1 teaspoon pure vanilla extract
1 cup sweetened flaked coconut
1 20-ounce can crushed pineapple in juice, well-drained

Topping
½ cup sweetened flaked coconut, toasted
1 10-ounce package frozen sliced strawberries in syrup, thawed
2 tablespoons whipping cream

Preheat oven to 325°.

Crust: Mix all crust ingredients in a bowl. Press mixture onto bottom of an ungreased 9-inch springform pan. Bake 10 minutes. Cool completely.

Filling: Beat cream cheese and 1 cup sugar in a large mixer bowl on medium speed until creamy. Beat in eggs, one at a time. Add sour cream, vanilla extract, 1 cup coconut and drained pineapple. Beat until well mixed. Spoon mixture into prepared pan. Bake 70–90 minutes or until set 2-inches from edge of pan.

Topping: Sprinkle with ¼ cup toasted coconut. Turn off oven and leave cheesecake in oven 2 hours with door slightly opened. Loosen sides of cheesecake from pan with a knife. Cover and immediately refrigerate. Chill 8 hours before serving. Sprinkle with remaining toasted coconut. Puree strawberries and strain in a bowl. Stir in 2 tablespoons cream. Top each serving with strawberry sauce as desired. Refrigerate leftovers.

Makes 12 servings.

WHITE CHOCOLATE CHEESECAKE
WITH STRAWBERRIES

For best flavor, use chocolate with cocoa butter listed in ingredients.

Crust
**1 9-ounce package chocolate
wafer cookies, finely ground
½ cup butter, melted**

Topping
**3 pints fresh strawberries, hulled
and halved
⅔ cup apricot preserves,
melted and strained, mixed with
⅛ teaspoon brandy extract**

Filling
**4 8-ounce packages cream cheese,
softened
1 pound quality white chocolate,
melted and cooled to lukewarm
1 cup granulated sugar
4 large eggs
1 cup dairy sour cream
½ cup whipping cream
2 tablespoons pure vanilla extract**

Preheat oven to 325°.
Butter a 10-inch springform pan. Wrap outside with foil.

Crust: Mix all crust ingredients in a bowl; press mixture onto bottom and
2-inches up sides of prepared pan. Bake 10 minutes. Cool on a wire rack.

Filling: Beat cream cheese in a large mixer bowl on medium speed until
fluffy. Gradually beat in sugar until smooth. Beat in eggs one at a time.
Beat in sour cream, whipping cream and vanilla extract until blended.
Gradually add melted white chocolate, beating until smooth. Pour mixture
into prepared crust. Bake until almost set, but center still has a slight jiggle
when pan is shaken, about 1 hour and 25 minutes. Turn oven off and leave
door slightly opened. Leave cheesecake in oven 30 minutes. Refrigerate
immediately; chill uncovered 8 hours. Remove sides of pan.

Topping: Arrange strawberries in circles covering top of cheesecake. Brush
with apricot mixture. Cut and serve. Refrigerate leftovers.

Makes 12 servings.

Cobblers
Crisps

BUSY DAY STRAWBERRY COBBLER

You can prepare this comfort dessert in minutes.

Filling
2 21-ounce cans strawberry pie filling
½ teaspoon ground cinnamon
½ teaspoon pure vanilla extract

⅓ cup cold butter
3 tablespoons whole milk
1 egg, slightly beaten

3 tablespoons granulated sugar

Topping
1½ cups all-purpose flour
2 tablespoons granulated sugar
1 teaspoon baking powder
½ teaspoon salt

Preheat oven to 400°.

Filling: Mix all filling ingredients in a large bowl until blended. Pour mixture into an ungreased 13x9-inch baking pan.

Topping: Mix flour, 2 tablespoons granulated sugar, baking powder and salt in a medium bowl. Cut in butter until crumbly with a pastry blender. Stir in milk and egg with a fork just until moistened. Spoon mixture over filling in pan. Sprinkle with 3 tablespoons granulated sugar. Bake 40–50 minutes or until gold brown and bubbly around edges. Serve warm in dessert bowls with light cream or vanilla ice cream. Refrigerate leftovers.

Makes 8 servings.

NECTARINE-STRAWBERRY COBBLER

Top with sweetened whipped cream when serving.

Filling
1¼ cups granulated sugar
1 tablespoon cornstarch
7 medium nectarines, pitted and
　sliced into ½-inch wedges
2 cups fresh strawberries
1 teaspoon pure vanilla extract

Topping
2 cups all-purpose flour
2 teaspoons baking powder
¾ teaspoon salt
10 tablespoons butter, cut into
　½-inch pieces
¾ cup whole milk

1 teaspoon granulated sugar mixed
　with pinch ground cinnamon

Preheat oven to 425°.
Butter a 2½ quart shallow baking dish.

Filling: Mix 1¼ cups sugar and cornstarch in a large bowl. Add nectarine
and strawberries; toss until coated. Spoon mixture into prepared baking
dish. Drizzle with vanilla. Bake until hot, about 10 minutes.

Topping: Mix flour, baking powder and salt in a large bowl. Cut in butter
with a pastry blender until mixture resembles coarse meal. Add milk; stir
just until dough forms. Drop dough onto hot fruit mixture in 6 mounds.
Sprinkle with sugar-cinnamon mixture. Bake 25–30 minutes. Serve slightly
warm. Refrigerate leftovers.

Makes 6 servings.

PEACH-STRAWBERRY-BLUEBERRY COBBLER

Fresh fruit is used in this tasty cobbler. Serve warm with a scoop of vanilla ice cream.

Filling
3 cups sliced fresh peaches
1 cup sliced fresh strawberries
1 cup fresh blueberries
2 teaspoons fresh lemon juice
1 teaspoon pure vanilla extract
⅓ cup granulated sugar mixed in
   a small bowl with 2 tablespoons
   all-purpose flour

Topping
¾ cup all-purpose flour
1 tablespoon granulated sugar
1½ teaspoons baking powder
¼ teaspoon salt
2 tablespoons cold butter, cut up
½ cup whipping cream
2 teaspoons granulated sugar

Preheat oven to 400°.
Butter a 9x9x2-inch baking dish or pan.

Filling: Mix all filling ingredients in a medium bowl until combined. Spoon mixture into prepared baking dish.

Topping: Mix flour, 1tablespoon sugar, baking powder and salt in a medium bowl. Cut in butter until mixture resembles small peas. Gradually stir in cream just until moistened. Drop dough by spoonfuls over filling. Sprinkle dough with 2 teaspoons sugar. Bake 20–25 minutes or until a wooden pick inserted into topping comes out clean. Refrigerate leftovers.

Makes 6 servings.

QUICK STRAWBERRY COBBLER

Frozen strawberries and a muffin mix are used in this sweet cobbler. Serve warm or cool with sweetened whipped cream.

Filling
½ cup granulated sugar
¼ cup cornstarch
2 10-ounce packages frozen sweetened sliced strawberries, thawed
1 teaspoon pure vanilla extract
2 tablespoons butter, cut into small pieces

Topping
1 7-ounce package raspberry muffin mix
¼ cup whole milk

Preheat oven to 425°.
Grease an 11x7x2-inch baking dish.

Filling: Mix sugar and cornstarch in a bowl. Stir in strawberries and vanilla extract until blended. Spoon mixture into prepared baking dish. Top evenly with butter.

Topping: Stir muffin mix and milk in a bowl just until blended. Drop dough by tablespoonfuls over strawberry mixture. Bake 18–24 minutes or until filling is bubbly and topping golden brown. Refrigerate leftovers.

Makes 6 servings.

RHUBARB-STRAWBERRY COBBLER

Rhubarb and strawberries… a perfect pair. Serve warm with vanilla ice cream or sweetened whipped cream.

Filling
1 cup granulated sugar
4 teaspoons cornstarch
2 tablespoons fresh orange juice
4 cups sliced fresh rhubarb
1 pint fresh strawberries, halved
1 teaspoon pure vanilla extract

Topping
1 cup all-purpose flour
2 tablespoons granulated sugar
1½ teaspoons baking powder
¼ teaspoon salt
¼ cup butter
1 egg mixed in a small bowl with
   2 tablespoons whole milk

Preheat oven to 400°.
Grease 2-quart baking dish.

Filling: Mix sugar and cornstarch in a large saucepan. Stir in orange juice. Add rhubarb. Cook and stir over medium heat until thickened and bubbly. Stir in strawberries and vanilla. Spoon mixture into baking dish.

Topping: Mix flour, 2 tablespoons, sugar, baking powder and salt in a bowl. Cut in butter until coarse crumbs form. Add egg mixture; stir only to moisten. Knead on a floured surface 6 times, and then roll dough out to an 11x4-inch rectangle. Cut dough lengthwise into ½-inch strips. Weave strips over hot fruit in baking dish to form a lattice; trim to fit. Place baking dish on a baking sheet to catch drips. Bake until fruit is tender and topping is golden, about 25 minutes.

Makes 8 servings.

STRAWBERRY COBBLER

Fresh strawberries are used in this cobbler. Serve warm with sweetened whipped cream or vanilla ice cream.

Filling
2 quarts fresh strawberries, halved
⅔ cup granulated sugar
¼ cup fresh orange juice
1 teaspoon pure vanilla extract
3 tablespoons quick-cooking tapioca
½ teaspoon ground cinnamon
¼ teaspoon ground nutmeg

Topping
1 cup all-purpose flour
5 tablespoons granulated sugar, divided
¼ teaspoon baking soda
¼ teaspoon salt
½ cup cold whole milk
¼ cup dairy sour cream
3 tablespoons butter, melted and cooled

Preheat oven to 350°.

Filling: Mix all filling ingredients in a large bowl. Spoon mixture into a 2-quart shallow baking dish.

Topping: Mix flour, 4 tablespoons granulated sugar, baking soda and salt in a medium bowl. Stir in milk, sour cream and butter until smooth. Drop dollops of mixture over fruit mixture. Sprinkle with 1 tablespoon granulated sugar. Bake about 35–40 minutes, until bubbly and topping is golden. Refrigerate leftovers.

Makes 6 servings.

NO-BAKE APRICOT-STRAWBERRY CRISP

When serving, top with thawed whipped topping...of course!

Filling
**1 17-ounce can apricot halves in heavy syrup, drained,
  reserving ½ cup syrup**
3 cups fresh strawberries, halved
½ teaspoon pure vanilla extract
¼ cup brown sugar, packed
2 teaspoons corn starch
½ teaspoon ground ginger

Topping
14 gingersnap cookies, coarsely crushed
1 tablespoon brown sugar
⅛ teaspoon ground cinnamon
2 tablespoons sliced almonds

Filling: Cut apricots in quarters; place in a medium bowl along with strawberries; set aside. Stir reserved syrup, ¼ cup brown sugar, cornstarch and ginger in a small saucepan over medium heat, stirring constantly, until mixture boils and is thickened. Stir mixture into apricot-strawberry mixture until blended. Spoon mixture into an 8x8-inch glass baking dish.

Topping: Mix all topping ingredients in a bowl. Sprinkle over filling mixture. Refrigerate and chill well. Refrigerate leftovers.

Makes 8 servings.

STRAWBERRY-RHUBARB CRISP

A crisp with fresh strawberries and fresh rhubarb…yummy. Serve warm with sweetened whipped cream or vanilla ice cream.

Filling
4 cups fresh strawberries, halved
3 cups fresh rhubarb,
 sliced ½-inch thick
1 teaspoon pure vanilla extract
⅔ cup granulated sugar
1 tablespoon cornstarch
1 tablespoon all-purpose flour

Topping
¾ cup all-purpose flour
¾ cup granulated sugar
½ teaspoon ground cinnamon
½ teaspoon ground nutmeg
⅛ teaspoon salt
6 tablespoons butter, softened
¾ cup quick-cooking oats,
 uncooked

Preheat oven to 400°.
Butter a shallow 2-quart baking dish.

Filling: Mix all filling ingredients in a large bowl until blended; set aside.

Topping: Mix flour, sugar, cinnamon, nutmeg and salt in another bowl. Cut in butter with a pastry blender until coarse crumbs form. Stir in quick-cooking oats. Spoon mixture evenly over filling mixture. Bake about 40 minutes or until bubbly and topping is lightly browned. Remove from oven. Cool slightly before serving. Refrigerate leftovers.

Makes 8 servings.

Desserts

A CHOCOLATE STRAWBERRY CUP

Red, white and blue...perfect for the July patio party!

½ cup crispy chow mein noodles
1 cup white chocolate chips

1 cup heavy whipping cream
1 tablespoon granulated sugar
1 teaspoon pure vanilla extract

1 cup fresh blueberries
3 cups fresh strawberries, sliced

Paper-line 12 muffin cups.

Spoon about 2 teaspoons chow mein noodles into each cup.
Melt chocolate following package directions; spoon about 1 tablespoon over noodles. Refrigerate until set, about 1 hour.

Beat whipping cream, sugar and vanilla extract in a mixer bowl with an electric mixer on medium speed to soft peaks. Gently fold in blueberries. Spoon equal amounts into each cup. Top each cup with strawberries and serve immediately. Refrigerate leftovers.

Makes 12 servings.

ALI'S STRAWBERRY COOKIE PARFAITS

A quick dessert to serve...pretty tasty too!

1 package (4-serving size) instant vanilla pudding and pie filling mix
2 cups whole cold milk

8 creme-filled golden sandwich cookies, coarsely chopped
2 cups sliced fresh strawberries
1 cup thawed non-dairy whipped topping

Beat pudding and milk in a medium bowl until blended, about 2 minutes.

Spoon 1 tablespoon chopped cookie crumbs into 6 dessert glasses. Spoon equal portions of pudding, then strawberries over cookie crumbs. Top each with whipped topping. Sprinkle with remaining cookie crumbs. Refrigerate and chill 1 hour before serving. Refrigerate leftovers.

Makes 6 servings.

ALMOND STRAWBERRY DACQUOISE

A dacquoise is a hard meringue made with ground nuts. This beauty is layered with berries and cream. Garnish with sliced strawberries.

Meringue
6 egg whites
¼ teaspoon cream of tartar
1 cup plus 2 tablespoons granulated sugar
½ cup ground blanched almonds
1 teaspoon almond extract

Filling
2 cups whipping cream
½ cup powdered sugar
4 cups strawberries, hulled
1½ teaspoons almond extract
¼ cup toasted chopped slivered almonds

Preheat oven to 275°.
Line two baking sheets with parchment paper; draw three 8-inch circles on paper.

Beat egg whites and cream of tartar in a large mixer bowl on high speed until foamy. Continue beating, gradually adding granulated sugar, until stiff and glossy, about 6–8 minutes. Fold in ground almonds and 1 teaspoon almond extract. Spoon meringue onto circles in prepared baking sheets; spread with back of a spoon to cover circles. Bake 60–75 minutes or until dry and firm to touch. Turn off oven and let dry 2 hours with door closed.

Beat whipping cream in a mixer bowl on high speed to soft peaks. Continue beating, gradually adding powdered sugar, to stiff peaks.

Mash half of the strawberries in a bowl; add 1½ teaspoons almond extract to strawberries. Fold mixture into whipped cream. Slice remaining strawberries; set aside.

Place one meringue on a serving plate; spread with one third filling. Top with half of sliced strawberries; repeat layering. Top with last meringue. Spread with remaining filling. Sprinkle chopped almonds around edge of top layer. Refrigerate 1 hour before serving. Refrigerate leftovers.

Makes 10 servings.

BANANA-STRAWBERRY ICE BOX DESSERT

This scrumptious dessert is so easy to prepare.

1 14-ounce can sweetened condensed milk
1 cup cold water
1 (4-serving size) package instant vanilla flavor pudding mix

2 cups whipping cream, stiffly whipped
2 cups fresh strawberries, sliced
2 bananas, sliced, dipped into lemon juice and drained
1 12-ounce prepared loaf pound cake, cut in 12 equal slices
additional fresh strawberries, sliced
additional sliced bananas dipped in lemon juice and drained

Mix sweetened condensed milk and water in a large bowl. Add dry pudding mix; beat well. Immediately refrigerate and chill 5 minutes.

Fold in whipped cream. Fold in 2 cups sliced strawberries and 2 sliced bananas. Line sides and bottom of a 3½-quart glass serving bowl with cake slices. Spoon pudding mixture into prepared bowl. Cover and immediately refrigerate; chill. Garnish top with a circle of additional strawberries and a circle of additional bananas. Refrigerate leftovers.

Makes 12 servings.

CHOCOLATE-DIPPED STRAWBERRIES

Chocolate strawberries…always a special treat.

4 cups fresh strawberries with stems
2 cups premier white chocolate chips
2 tablespoons solid shortening, divided
  (do not use butter, margarine or oil)
1 cup semi-sweet chocolate chips

rinsed strawberries; patted dry and chilled

Line a baking sheet with waxed paper.

Place white chips and 1 tablespoon shortening in a medium microwave-safe bowl. Microwave on high 1 minute; stir until chips are melted and mixture is smooth. Holding by the top, dip two thirds of each strawberry into mixture; shake gently to remove excess. Place on prepared baking sheet. Refrigerate until firm, at least 30 minutes.

Repeat microwave procedure with semi-sweet chocolate chips and remaining 1 tablespoon shortening in a clean microwave-safe bowl. Dip lower third of each strawberry into mixture. Place on baking sheet. Cover with waxed paper. Refrigerate until set, about 30 minutes.

Makes about 2 dozen servings.

CHOCOLATE MALLOW FONDUE WITH STRAWBERRY DIPPERS

Give each guest a fork…remember no double-dipping!

Fondue
2 cups semi-sweet chocolate chips
1 14-ounce can sweetened condensed milk
1 7-ounce jar marshmallow crème
½ cup whole milk
1 teaspoon pure vanilla extract

Dippers
fresh strawberries
cubed pound cake
banana chunks
marshmallows

Fondue: Mix first five ingredients in a 2-quart heavy saucepan. Cook over low heat, stirring often, until just until melted; whisk until smooth. Pour fondue into a fondue pot, chafing dish or small slow cooker; keep warm.

To serve, dip dippers, one piece at a time, in warm fondue, using fondue forks, chopsticks or long wooden skewers. Refrigerate leftovers.

Makes about 4 cups.

CHOCOLATE STRAWBERRY ÉCLAIR

A beautiful dessert that tastes just like a regular size éclair.

Shell
¾ cup water
6 tablespoons butter or
   margarine
¾ cup all-purpose flour
⅛ teaspoon salt
3 large eggs

Filling
1½ cups semi-sweet
   chocolate chips, divided

3 tablespoons whole milk
2 teaspoons pure vanilla extract, divided
1 8-ounce package light cream cheese,
   softened
½ cup powdered sugar
15 large strawberries, hulled and tops
   trimmed level
⅓ cup seedless raspberry jam, melted
1¾ cups frozen nondairy whipped topping,
   thawed

Preheat oven to 450°.
Grease a 9-inch pie plate.

Shell: Heat water and butter to a boil in a small saucepan. Stir in flour and salt. Reduce heat to low and stir vigorously for 1 minute or until mixture forms a ball. Remove from heat. Cool 3 minutes. Add eggs one at a time mixing thoroughly after each addition, until smooth. Spread dough evenly over bottom of prepared pie plate. Bake 15 minutes or until sides puff up. Reduce heat to 350° and bake 10 minutes or until golden brown. Cool completely in pie plate on a wire rack. Press center down when cool.

Filling: Microwave 1¼ cups chips and milk uncovered in a microwave-safe bowl on high 1 minute. Stir until smooth. Do not overheat. Stir in 1 teaspoon vanilla extract. Spread mixture evenly over shell. Chill until firm. Beat cream cheese, powdered sugar and 1 teaspoon vanilla extract in a small bowl until smooth; spread evenly over chocolate layer. Place strawberries pointed side up, over cheese layer, leaving a space around shell. Brush strawberries with jam. Spoon dollops of whipped topping between strawberries and shell. Melt remaining chocolate chips; drizzle over strawberries. Serve immediately. Refrigerate leftovers.

Makes 8 servings.

CREAM CHEESE CHOCOLATE-FILLED STRAWBERRY MERINGUES

Delicate meringue shells filled with creamy chocolate filling and topped with strawberry sauce.

Meringues
2 egg whites
¼ teaspoon cream of tartar
¼ teaspoon pure vanilla extract
⅛ teaspoon salt
½ cup granulated sugar

1 10-ounce package frozen sweetened sliced strawberries, thawed

Filling
1 8-ounce package cream cheese, softened
1 cup powdered sugar
¼ cup unsweetened cocoa powder
½ teaspoon pure vanilla extract
1 cup thawed whipping topping

Preheat oven to 300°.
Line a baking sheet with parchment paper.

Meringues: Place egg whites in a small mixer bowl; let stand at room temperature 30 minutes. Beat with an electric mixer on medium until foamy. Add cream of tartar, ¼ teaspoon vanilla extract and salt; beat until soft peaks form. Gradually add granulated sugar, 1 tablespoon at a time, beating until stiff peaks form. Spoon meringue into six mounds on paper. Shape each into 3-inch shell using the back of a spoon. Bake 35 minutes. Turn oven off and do not open door. Let meringues dry in oven 1 hour. Cool on a wire rack.

Filling: Beat cream cheese with an electric mixer in a bowl until fluffy. Add powdered sugar, cocoa powder and ½ teaspoon vanilla extract; beat until smooth. Fold in whipped topping.

Puree strawberries in food processor. To serve, spoon filling into cooled meringue shell. Top each with strawberry puree. Refrigerate leftovers.

Makes 6 servings.

CREAMY PINEAPPLE-STRAWBERRY REFRIGERATED DESSERT

Cream cheese, pineapple and strawberries in a tasty crust.

Crust
1½ cups all-purpose flour
1 cup butter or margarine, softened
½ cup powdered sugar
½ cup almonds, very finely chopped

Filling
1 8-ounce package cream cheese,
   softened
⅔ cup granulated sugar
1 teaspoon pure vanilla extract

1 20-ounce can crushed pineapple,
   drained, reserving 1 cup juice
1½ cups heavy whipping cream,
   stiffly whipped in a bowl
2 cups miniature marshmallows

Topping
1 tablespoon cornstarch
1 cup reserved pineapple juice
½ cup reserved pineapple
1 cup ripe sliced strawberries

Preheat oven to 400°.

Crust: Beat flour, butter and powdered sugar with an electric mixer in a large bowl on low speed 1 minute. Beat on high speed until creamy, about 2 minutes. Stir in almonds. Spread dough into an ungreased 13x9x2-inch baking pan. Bake until golden brown, about 14 minutes. Cool completely.

Filling: Beat cream cheese, granulated sugar and vanilla extract with an electric mixer in a large bowl until fluffy. Reserve ½ cup pineapple; stir remaining pineapple into cream cheese mixture. Fold in whipped cream and marshmallows. Spoon mixture into crust. Cover and refrigerate until well chilled. Cut into squares. Serve with topping. Refrigerate leftovers.

Topping: Place cornstarch in a medium saucepan. Gradually stir in pineapple juice. Cook over medium heat, stirring constantly, until mixture boils and is thickened. Boil and stir 1 minute. Cool. Fold in ½ cup pineapple and 1 cup strawberries. Refrigerate leftovers.

Makes 12 servings.

FRESH STRAWBERRY CREAM CHEESE SQUARES

The prepared strawberry glaze (usually found by the fresh strawberries) makes a delicious topping for this creamy bar.

Crust
2 cups all-purpose biscuit baking mix
2 tablespoons granulated sugar
½ cup butter or margarine, softened
⅓ cup warm water

Filling
1 8-ounce package cream cheese, softened
1 14-ounce can sweetened condensed milk
⅓ cup lemon juice
1 teaspoon pure vanilla extract

Topping
4 cups fresh strawberries, rinsed, hulled and sliced
1 16-ounce container prepared strawberry glaze, chilled
1 8-ounce container frozen nondairy whipped topping, thawed

Preheat oven to 400°.
Lightly grease a 9-inch square baking pan.

Crust: Mix biscuit mix and sugar in a medium bowl. Add butter and water. Beat until well blended. Pour mixture into prepared pan; with floured hands, press evenly over bottom. Bake 10–12 minutes or until lightly browned. Remove from oven; cool in pan.

Filling: Beat cream cheese in a large mixer bowl with an electric mixer until fluffy. Gradually beat in sweetened condensed milk until smooth. Beat in lemon juice and vanilla extract. Spread mixture over cooled crust in pan. Refrigerate immediately and chill at least 3 hours, before serving. Cut into squares.

Topping: When serving, mix strawberries and glaze in a bowl. Spoon mixture over each serving. Top each with whipped topping as desired. Refrigerate leftovers.

Makes 8 servings.

LEMON CURD STRAWBERRY PIZZA

Lemon curd holds fresh fruit on a cookie crust...you'll love it!

1 18-ounce package refrigerated sugar cookie dough

2 tablespoons strawberry jam, melted
¾ cup lemon curd, purchase or use the recipe below
2 cups sliced fresh strawberries
2 cups fresh raspberries
1 cup fresh blackberries
2 teaspoons granulated sugar

Preheat oven to 350°.
Coat a 12-inch pizza pan with cooking spray.

Press dough into prepared pan. Bake until golden brown, about 12 minutes.
Remove from oven; cool completely on a wire rack.
Preheat broiler.

Spread jam over cooled crust. Top evenly with lemon curd. Place berries
over lemon curd. Sprinkle with 2 teaspoons sugar. Broil 3 minutes. Serve.
Refrigerate leftovers.

Lemon Curd: Mix ¾ cup granulated sugar, 1 tablespoon freshly grated
lemon rind and 2 large eggs in a saucepan. Cook and stir over medium
heat until mixture is light in color, about 3 minutes. Stir in ⅔ cup fresh
lemon juice and 2 tablespoons butter; cook and stir with a whisk about
5 minutes or until mixture coats back of a spoon. Cool completely. Cover
and store in refrigerator up to 1 week.

Makes 12 servings.

LEMON-STRAWBERRY ANGEL DESSERT

Purchased angel food cake makes this beautiful dessert easy to prepare ahead of time.

4 ounces cream cheese, softened (half of 8-ounce package)
1 cup lemon yogurt
2 cups cold milk
1 package (3.4-ounces) instant lemon pudding mix
2 teaspoons freshly grated lemon peel

2½ cups sliced fresh strawberries, divided
1 tablespoon water
1 10-inch prepared angel food cake

Beat cream cheese and yogurt in a medium bowl until blended. Add milk, dry pudding mix and lemon peel; beat until smooth.

Puree ½ cup strawberries with water in a blender; set aside.

Tear cake into 1-inch pieces; place one third into a 3-quart glass serving bowl or trifle bowl. Top with one third of pudding mixture and half of the remaining sliced strawberries. Drizzle with half of the strawberry puree. Repeat. Top with remaining cake and pudding mixture. Cover and immediately refrigerate. Chill for at least 2 hours before serving. Scoop into dessert dishes and garnish each with a fresh strawberry. Refrigerate leftovers.

Makes 14 servings.

LEMONY STRAWBERRY CHEESECAKE SQUARES

Cream cheese, strawberry preserves and lemon…yummy.

Crust
2 cups vanilla wafer cookie crumbs
¼ cup granulated sugar
½ cup butter, melted

Filling
¾ cup strawberry preserves
3 8-ounce packages cream cheese, softened
1 14-ounce can sweetened condensed milk
3 eggs
½ cup fresh lemon juice
½ teaspoon pure vanilla extract

Preheat oven to 375°.

Crust: Mix all crust ingredients in a bowl; press mixture firmly onto bottom of a 13x9x2-inch baking pan. Bake 8 minutes. Remove from oven. Cool.

Reduce oven temperature to 300°.

Filling: Spread strawberry preserves evenly over prepared crust. Beat cream cheese with an electric mixer in a larger bowl until fluffy. Gradually beat in sweetened condensed milk until smooth. Beat in eggs, lemon juice and vanilla extract until well mixed; pour mixture over strawberry preserves. Bake about 45–50 minutes or until center is set. Remove from oven. Cool, then refrigerate and chill well before serving. Garnish with sweetened whipped cream as desired. Refrigerate leftovers.

Makes 12 servings.

LOLA'S STRAWBERRY ANGEL DESSERT

This luscious recipe comes from St. Anthony Village, Minnesota.

1 angel food cake, purchased or homemade
1 6-ounce package strawberry-flavored gelatin
2½ cups hot water
2 10-ounce packages frozen sweetened strawberries
1 pint whipping cream

Topping
1 cup whipping cream whipped in a medium bowl with
   2 tablespoons powdered sugar and ⅛ teaspoon almond extract.

Break angel food cake into chunks and place into a large buttered 13x9-inch glass baking dish.

Dissolve gelatin in hot water in a bowl. Add frozen strawberries. Refrigerate and let set until a syrupy consistency is formed.

Whip the cream in another bowl and fold into partially set gelatin mixture. Pour mixture over cake in baking dish. Refrigerate immediately and let chill overnight. When serving top with almond-flavored whipped cream as desired. Refrigerate leftovers.

Makes 12 servings.

MERINGUES WITH STRAWBERRIES AND CREAM

Meringues filled with strawberries and cream…a good dessert.

3 large egg whites
¼ teaspoon cream of tartar
1 cup granulated sugar
1 teaspoon ground cinnamon
½ teaspoon baking powder

10 2-inch square saltine crackers, coarsely crushed
½ cup chopped walnuts
6 cups fresh strawberries, sliced and sweetened to taste
sweetened whipped cream

Preheat oven to 300°.
Line two baking sheets with cooking parchment paper or lightly oil nonstick baking sheets.

Beat egg whites and cream of tartar in a large bowl with an electric mixer on high speed until foamy. Mix sugar, cinnamon and baking powder in a bowl; gradually beat into egg whites on high speed and continue beating until stiff glossy peaks are formed.

Fold in crackers and walnuts. Spoon mixture in eight equal mounds about 3½-inches wide, well separated, onto prepared baking sheets. Bake until lightly browned, about 30 minutes. Remove from oven; cool on baking sheets 10 minutes, then transfer meringues to cooling racks.

Mix strawberries with sweetened whipped cream in a bowl. Spoon over meringues when serving. Refrigerate leftovers.

Makes 8 servings.

107

MR. BROWN'S KIWI-STRAWBERRY ANGEL DESSERT

Tangy lime, angel food cake, kiwi fruit and saucy strawberries in this luscious dessert...just like Mr. Brown, total delight.

10 cups cubed angel food cake, divided
2 6-ounce containers vanilla yogurt
2 teaspoons grated fresh lime peel
¼ cup fresh lime juice
1 8-ounce container frozen nondairy whipped topping, thawed
6 medium size kiwi fruit, peeled and sliced
1 24-ounce package frozen unsweetened whole strawberries, thawed and reserving juice

2 tablespoons granulated sugar
1 tablespoon cornstarch
½ teaspoon pure vanilla extract

Place 5 cups angel food cubes in an ungreased 13x9x2-inch glass baking dish. Mix yogurt, lime peel and juice in a large bowl. Fold in whipped topping. Spread half the mixture over cake cubes in baking dish. Press down until an even layer is formed. Arrange kiwi over cake layer. Top with remaining cake cubes; press, then top with remaining yogurt mixture. Cover and refrigerate until thoroughly chilled, at least 3 hours.

Mash strawberries in a saucepan. Bring to a boil over medium heat. Mix 2 tablespoons sugar, cornstarch and reserved juice in a small bowl; stir mixture into strawberries. Cook, stirring constantly, until thickened, about 2 minutes. Remove from heat; stir in vanilla. Refrigerate until serving. Serve cake topped with strawberry sauce. Refrigerate leftovers.

Makes 10 servings.

STRAWBERRY CREAM PUFFS

Puffs...delicate and delicious. For variation, fill puffs with softened vanilla ice cream mixed with sliced strawberries.

Dough
1 cup water
½ cup butter
1 teaspoon granulated sugar
¼ teaspoon salt
1 cup all-purpose flour
4 eggs

Filling
2 pints fresh strawberries, sliced, mixed in a bowl with ¼ cup granulated sugar and chilled 30 minutes
2 cups whipping cream
¼ cup granulated sugar
½ teaspoon pure vanilla extract

Preheat oven to 400°.
Grease a baking sheet.

Dough: Bring water, butter, 1 teaspoon sugar and salt to a boil in a large saucepan. Add flour all at once and stir immediately until a smooth ball forms. Remove from heat; let stand 5 minutes. Beat in eggs, one at a time, and continue beating until mixture is smooth and shiny. Drop dough by 12 rounded table spoonfuls 3 inches apart onto prepared baking sheet. Bake 30–35 minutes or until golden brown. Remove from baking sheet; cool on a wire rack. Immediately cut a slit in each puff to vent steam. Cool. Split puffs; set tops aside. Remove soft dough from inside with a fork. Cool puffs completely.

Filling: Beat whipping cream in a bowl with ¼ cup sugar and ½ teaspoon vanilla until stiff. Fold in chilled strawberries. Fill cream puffs with creamy strawberry mixture; replace caps. Serve. Refrigerate leftovers.

Makes 12 servings.

STRAWBERRY BAVARIAN CREAM

This recipe comes from Houston, Texas…thanks, Cousin Jane!

1 cup whole milk

1 envelope unflavored gelatin (¼-ounce)
2 tablespoons cold water
½ cup granulated sugar
1 8-ounce container dairy sour cream
½ teaspoon almond extract

1 10-ounce package frozen sliced strawberries in syrup, thawed

Heat milk in a 2-quart saucepan over medium heat until it just comes to a boil, about 5–7 minutes.

Sprinkle gelatin over water in a small bowl; let stand 5 minutes to soften. Add gelatin and sugar to milk; stir until dissolved. Cool to room temperature, about 30 minutes. Whisk in sour cream and almond extract until smooth. Pour mixture into a 1-quart mold. Cover and refrigerate until set, about 2–3 hours. Un-mold on a serving plate. Top with strawberries and serve. Store in refrigerator.

Makes 8 servings.

STRAWBERRY BREAD PUDDING

Garnish with sliced fresh strawberries and sweetened whipped cream or thawed whipped topping when serving.

Pudding
**1 loaf day-old French bread, broken
 in pieces to make 8 cups**
2 cups heavy cream
2 cups granulated sugar
3 large eggs
½ cup butter, melted
2 tablespoons pure vanilla extract
1 teaspoon ground cinnamon
½ teaspoon ground nutmeg
1 cup pureed strawberries

Sauce
½ cup butter
1½ cups powdered sugar
1 egg, beaten
½ cup pureed strawberries

Preheat oven to 350°.
Butter a 9x9-inch baking dish.

Pudding: Mix all pudding ingredients in a large bowl. Pour mixture into prepared baking dish. Place on middle rack of oven. Bake about 1 hour and 15 minutes and top is golden brown.

Sauce: Mix butter and powdered sugar in a saucepan over medium heat, stirring constantly, until well blended. Stir in egg, a little at a time; cook and stir 2 minutes, do not boil. Remove from heat. Stir in pureed strawberries. Serve warm over warm pudding. Refrigerate leftovers.

Makes 8 servings.

STRAWBERRY CHEESECAKE TRIFLE

Garnish with fresh strawberries when serving.

4 cups fresh strawberries, sliced
½ cup granulated sugar
3 tablespoon fresh orange juice

2 8-ounce packages cream cheese, softened
½ cup granulated sugar
3 tablespoons fresh orange juice
3 cups whipping cream, whipped with 3 tablespoons
   powdered sugar and 1 teaspoon pure vanilla extract

1 10-ounce frozen pound cake, thawed and
   cubed into ½-inch pieces
3 ounces semi-sweet chocolate, grated

Mix strawberries and ½ cup granulated sugar in a bowl; let set 1 hour or until juice forms. Drain and reserve juice in a bowl; add orange juice.

Beat cream cheese and ½ cup granulated sugar in a large mixer bowl until smooth. Fold in whipped cream.

Toss cake cubes with reserved strawberry juice mixture in a large bowl. Layer half the mixture into a 4-quart trifle dish or a large glass serving bowl. Top with a third of cream cheese mixture, then half the drained strawberries and half the grated chocolate. Repeat layers. Top with remaining cream cheese. Refrigerate immediately; cover and chill overnight before serving. Refrigerate leftovers.

Makes 12 servings.

STRAWBERRY DESSERT PIZZA

A good dessert for that patio party…add other fresh fruit if desired.

1 20-ounce package refrigerated sugar cookie dough

1 8-ounce package cream cheese, softened
⅓ cup granulated sugar
1 teaspoon pure vanilla extract
1 container frozen non-dairy whipped topping, thawed

2 cups fresh strawberries, sliced

melted white chocolate

Preheat oven to 350°.
Grease a 12-inch pizza pan.

Press cookie dough firmly into prepared pan. Bake 20 minutes or until golden brown. Remove from oven; cool in pan on a wire rack.

Beat cream cheese, sugar and vanilla extract in a large bowl on high speed until well blended. Gently stir in whipped topping. Spread mixture over cooled crust.

Top with strawberries. Drizzle with melted white chocolate as desired. Cut into wedges and serve immediately or cover and refrigerate until ready to serve. Refrigerate leftovers.

Makes 12 servings.

RHUBARB-STRAWBERRY TRIFLE

Garnish this tempting dessert with fresh whole strawberries.

2 cups fresh rhubarb cut into ½-inch
    pieces or unsweetened frozen
    rhubarb, thawed and drained
1 cup granulated sugar
¼ cup fresh orange juice or water
1 teaspoon pure vanilla extract
2 cups sliced strawberries

2 4-serving size packages cook and
    serve vanilla pudding mix
2½ cups whole milk

1 cup heavy whipping cream,
    whipped to stiff peaks with
    2 tablespoons granulated sugar
    and ½ teaspoon pure vanilla
    extract

1 16-ounce package frozen pound
    cake loaf
½ cup orange marmalade or
    strawberry jam

Bring rhubarb, 1 cup sugar and orange juice to a boil in a 2-quart
saucepan over medium heat. Reduce heat; cook stirring occasionally until
rhubarb is tender and slightly thickened. Stir in 1 teaspoon vanilla extract.
Remove from heat; cool 30 minutes. Refrigerate; chill. Stir in strawberries.

Cook pudding and milk in a 2-quart saucepan over medium heat, stirring
constantly, until mixture boils. Remove from heat; cool in pan 15 minutes,
then chill well in refrigerator. Fold in whipped cream.

Cut pound cake horizontally in half. Spread marmalade over bottom half.
Top with top half. Cut into 18 slices. Place 9 slices in bottom of a 3-quart
glass serving bowl. Spoon half the rhubarb mixture over cake; top with half
the pudding. Repeat layers with remaining cake, rhubarb and pudding.
Cover and refrigerate until well chilled. Refrigerate leftovers.

Makes 12 servings.

STRAWBERRY NAPOLEONS

Serve these for a special occasion.

1 17-ounce package frozen puff
  pastry, thawed
½ cup powdered sugar

½ cup heavy cream
½ cup crème fraiche

1 vanilla bean, halved lengthwise,
  seeds scraped and reserved
2 tablespoons powdered sugar
2 pints fresh strawberries,
  stemmed and sliced

Preheat oven to 350°.

Unfold puff pastry; place on two baking sheets. Bake until dough is puffed but is still soft and not browned, about 7–10 minutes. Set a wire rack on top of dough and press gently to flatten to ⅛-inch thickness. Bake until lightly browned, about 8 minutes. Cool on a clean wire rack. Increase oven temperature to 425°.

Carefully cut pastry with a serrated knife into 18 2x3-inch rectangles. Dust each evenly with ½ cup powdered sugar. Bake until browned and sugar forms a glaze, about 2–3 minutes. Remove from oven. Cool on a rack.

Whisk heavy cream, crème fraiche, vanilla seeds and 2 tablespoons powdered sugar in a medium mixing bowl until stiff. Place mixture into a disposable pastry bag. Cut ½-inch from tip of bag. Pipe ¼-inch thick layer of mixture over 12 pastry rectangles. Top each with a single layer of strawberries. Stack six filled pastries, face up, on top of the other six. Top each stack with one of the remaining plain pastries. Refrigerate leftovers.

Makes 6 servings.

STRAWBERRY RHUBARB FOOL

Cooked fruit, folded in whipped cream and layered with fresh fruit is defined as "fool"…you'll love this rhubarb laden strawberry fool!

3 cups sliced rhubarb, fresh or frozen
⅓ cup granulated sugar
¼ cup fresh orange juice
⅛ teaspoon salt, scant
½ teaspoon pure vanilla extract

1 cup whipping cream
2 cups fresh strawberries, halved

additional fresh sliced strawberries

Mix first four ingredients in a medium saucepan. Bring to a boil, then reduce heat; cover and simmer until rhubarb is tender, about 6 minutes. Remove from heat; stir in vanilla extract. Cool slightly. Pour into a blender; process until smooth. Pour mixture into a large bowl; chill.

Just before serving, whip cream in a medium bowl until stiff peaks form. Fold into rhubarb mixture until lightly streaked. Place alternate layers of rhubarb-cream mixture and halved strawberries in chilled dessert glasses. Garnish with sliced strawberries as desired. Refrigerate leftovers.

Makes 6 servings.

STRAWBERRIES ROMANOFF

An easy way to enjoy a strawberry classic.

1 pint strawberries, washed, halved
¼ cup fresh orange juice
¼ cup orange-flavored liqueur

1 cup heavy whipping cream, well chilled
2 tablespoons granulated sugar

Place strawberries in a large bowl. Combine orange juice and liqueur; pour over strawberries. Cover and refrigerate 1 hour.

Beat cream in a mixer bowl on medium-high speed until soft peaks form. Add sugar and continue beating until firm peaks form, about 2 minutes. Spoon strawberries into dessert glasses; top with whipped cream. Refrigerate leftovers.

Makes 4 servings.

STRAWBERRY TRUFFLES

Special candy...for special friends.

5-ounces white chocolate (with cocoa butter listed in ingredients)

1 8-ounce package cream cheese, softened
4 cups powdered sugar
1 teaspoon freshly grated ginger root

18 medium fresh strawberries
¼ cup finely minced crystallized ginger
½ cup toasted coconut
½ cup finely chopped pistachio nuts

Melt white chocolate in the top of a double boiler; cool.

Beat cream cheese, sugar and ginger root in a bowl on medium speed until smooth. Add cooled melted chocolate; mix well. Chill until easy to handle, about 1 hour.

Scoop out pulp of each strawberry with a small spoon halfway down center; pat dry. Put a small amount of crystallized ginger into each strawberry. Shape cheese mixture around each strawberry, then dip one end in the coconut and other end in pistachio nuts. Place truffles in paper candy cups. Chill until ready to serve. Refrigerate leftovers.

Makes about 18.

STRAWBERRIES WITH CREAMY VANILLA CUSTARD

Variation: Include other fresh berries, such as raspberries and blueberries…serve this delicious homemade custard warm or cool.

1½ cups heavy whipping cream

½ cup granulated sugar
1 tablespoon cornstarch
4 egg yolks
2 teaspoons pure vanilla extract
fresh strawberries, hulled

Heat whipping cream in a 2-quart saucepan over medium until cream just comes to a boil, about 6 minutes. Remove from heat.

Mix sugar and cornstarch in a medium bowl until blended. Add egg yolks and whisk with a wire whisk until light and creamy, about 3 minutes. Gradually whisk hot cream into egg yolk mixture.

Return mixture to same saucepan. Stir in vanilla. Cook over medium heat, stirring constantly, until custard is thickened and coats back of a metal spoon, about 4 minutes (do not boil). Remove from heat; cool slightly. Serve over fresh strawberries. Refrigerate leftovers.

Makes 8 servings.

THE GIRL'S NO-BAKE STRAWBERRY ANGEL DESSERT

The girls always top it with a little whipped cream...of course!

1 purchased 10-inch angel food cake, crumbled

2 8-ounce packages cream cheese, softened
1 teaspoon pure vanilla extract
1 cup granulated sugar
1 8-ounce container frozen nondairy whipped topping, thawed

1 quart fresh ripe strawberries, hulled and sliced
1 18-ounce jar strawberry glaze

Place crumbled cake into a 13x9x2-inch glass baking dish; press down with hands to make a single layer.

Beat cream cheese with an electric mixer in a medium bowl until fluffy. Beat in vanilla and sugar until smooth. Fold in whipped topping; spread mixture over cake layer.

Mix fresh strawberries and strawberry glaze in a bowl until well coated; spread over cream cheese layer. Refrigerate and chill well before serving. Refrigerate leftovers.

Makes 16 servings.

WHITE CAKE MIX STRAWBERRY DELIGHT

White cake covered with cream cheese and whipped cream, then topped with a thick strawberry glaze.

1 18.25-ounce white cake mix
4 ounces cream cheese, softened
1 cup powdered sugar
½ teaspoon pure vanilla extract
1 cup whipping cream, whipped

1 16-ounce container strawberry glaze
½ cup water
2½ cups fresh or frozen unsweetened sliced strawberries

Prepare and bake cake mix according to package directions, using a 13x9x2-inch baking pan. Cool on a wire rack.

Beat cream cheese and powdered sugar in a large bowl until smooth. Beat in vanilla extract. Fold in whipped cream. Spread mixture over cooled cake. Refrigerate until ready to serve.

Just before serving, mix strawberry glaze and water in a medium bowl; fold in strawberries. Spoon over each serving. Refrigerate leftovers.

Makes 12 servings.

WHITE CHOCOLATE STRAWBERRY FROSTY BERRY MELANGE

White chocolate melted in cream and spooned over frosty assorted berries…a delightful dessert prepared in minutes.

1¼ pounds high quality white chocolate, coarsely chopped (the kind with cocoa butter listed in the ingredients)
2½ cups heavy cream
2 tablespoons pure vanilla extract

2 cups frozen mixed berries
1 cup frozen strawberries
1 cup frozen blueberries
1 cup frozen raspberries

Place chopped chocolate, cream and vanilla in top of a double boiler. Heat over simmering water until chocolate melts; stir and keep warm.

Portion frozen berries in individual shallow dessert bowls 6 minutes before serving. Spoon warm chocolate over berries and serve immediately.

Makes 8 servings.

WHITE CHOCOLATE TIRAMISU WITH STRAWBERRIES AND RASPBERRIES

Tiramisu individually portioned… an elegant dessert.

½ cup whole milk
4 ounces quality white chocolate,
   broken into small pieces

¼ cup granulated sugar
8 ounces mascarpone cheese
¾ cup heavy whipping cream
1 teaspoon pure vanilla extract

16 thin slices sponge or angel food cake spooned evenly with
   ¼ cup raspberry flavored syrup or raspberry liqueur
4 tablespoons grated bittersweet or semi-sweet chocolate
8 whole fresh strawberries, hulled and sliced
6 ounces fresh raspberries

Heat milk in a saucepan over medium-low heat until bubbles form around edges of saucepan; pour over white chocolate in a small bowl; whisk until chocolate is completely melted; cool.

Beat sugar and mascarpone in a medium bowl. Whisk in white chocolate mixture. Whip heavy whipping cream and vanilla extract to soft peaks in another bowl; fold into mascarpone mixture.

Place 1 cake slice each in bottom of 8 tall dessert glasses. Spoon half the cream mixture over cake slice. Sprinkle each with ½ tablespoon grated chocolate; top with 1 sliced strawberry. Repeat layers, cake, cream and grated chocolate. Refrigerate immediately; chill 4 hours before serving. Top with fresh raspberries when serving. Refrigerate leftovers.

Makes 8 servings.

ZABAGLIONE WITH FRESH STRAWBERRIES

Save this one for a special dinner.

7 large egg yolks
½ cup granulated sugar
⅛ teaspoon salt
¾ cup Chardonnay
2 tablespoons orange-flavored liqueur

4 cups ripe sliced strawberries

Beat egg yolks, sugar and salt in a bowl until light. Place mixture in top of a double boiler over simmering water; whisk in Chardonnay and orange-flavored liqueur. Continue whisking until the mixture mounds and quadruples in volume, about 3 minutes. Mixture should be the consistency of lightly whipped cream, with no liquid visible.

Serve immediately spooned over top of strawberries in dessert glasses. Refrigerate leftovers.

Makes 6 servings.

Frozen Desserts

BARBARA MADISON'S FROZEN STRAWBERRY DESSERT

Use only pasteurized eggs when preparing this delicious dessert. There was a time one could safely use regular raw eggs, but because of the danger of salmonella, pasteurized eggs are recommended when raw eggs are used in any recipe.

Crust
1 cup all-purpose flour
½ cup margarine
¼ cup brown sugar
½ cup nuts, chopped

½ cup granulated sugar
1 10-ounce package frozen sliced strawberries in juice
2 tablespoons lemon juice

Filling
2 pasteurized egg whites
1 8-ounce container nondairy frozen whipped topping, thawed

Preheat oven to 350°.

Crust: Mix all crust ingredients in a bowl until well blended. Pat mixture into a 13x9-inch baking pan to form a crust. Bake 20 minutes. Remove from oven. Cool completely in pan on a wire rack.

Filling: Beat egg whites with an electric mixer in a large bowl until stiff like meringue. Beat in non-dairy whipped topping. Add sugar and continue beating until well blended. Add strawberries and lemon juice and stir lightly to combine. Place mixture into the cooled baked crust and freeze. Take out at least 1 hour before serving. Freeze leftovers.

Makes 10 servings.

COOKIE-CRUSTED STRAWBERRY FREEZE

Chocolate chip cookies, cream cheese and strawberries in this frosty dessert.

12 chocolate chip cookies, purchased or homemade
1 8-ounce package cream cheese, softened
½ cup granulated sugar
1 12-ounce can frozen berry juice concentrate, thawed
½ teaspoon pure vanilla extract
1 cup crushed strawberries
1 8-ounce container frozen nondairy whipped topping, thawed

2 cups whole strawberries, halved

Place cookies on bottom of a 9-inch springform pan.

Beat cream cheese and sugar in a large bowl with an electric mixer on medium speed until well blended. Gradually beat in juice concentrate. Add vanilla extract and crushed strawberries; mix well. Stir in whipped topping with a wire whisk until well blended. Pour mixture over cookies in pan. Freeze until firm. Let stand at room temperature 10 minutes before serving. Top with halved strawberries when serving. Freeze leftovers.

Makes 16 servings.

CREAMY STRAWBERRY FROZEN YOGURT

Use fresh or frozen strawberries in this creamy yogurt.

½ **cup granulated sugar**
2 **teaspoons cornstarch**

1 **cup whipping cream**
¼ **cup light corn syrup**
1 **egg, slightly beaten in a cup**

2 **cups unsweetened strawberries, pureed until smooth**
½ **teaspoon pure vanilla extract**
1 **cup plain low-fat yogurt**

Mix sugar and cornstarch in a medium saucepan. Stir in whipping cream and corn syrup until blended. Cook over medium heat, stirring constantly, until mixture simmers; stir a small amount of mixture in egg, then stir the egg mixture into saucepan. Cook and stir over medium-low heat 3 minutes. Pour mixture into a bowl and cool completely.

Stir in vanilla extract and yogurt. Pour mixture into freezer can of an ice cream maker. Freeze according to the manufacturer's instructions. Serve or store in freezer container in the freezer.

Makes 1 quart.

EASY STRAWBERRY ICE CREAM

Easy to make…enjoy this homemade cool treat.

4 cups half and half
1 14-ounce can sweetened condensed milk
2½ teaspoons pure vanilla extract
2 cups mashed fresh or frozen strawberries, thawed

Mix all ingredients in a large bowl. Pour into the freezer can of an ice cream maker. Freeze according to the manufacturer's instructions. Serve or freeze leftovers.

Makes about 1½ quarts.

FRESH STRAWBERRY SORBET

For a firmer texture place frozen sorbet into an airtight container and place in the freezer until firm.

1 cup granulated sugar
1 cup cold water

1 quart fresh strawberries, quartered
4 tablespoons fresh lemon juice
¼ cup corn syrup

Bring sugar and water to a boil in a medium saucepan. Reduce heat and simmer without stirring until sugar is completely dissolved. Pour mixture into a bowl and cool completely.

Process strawberries and lemon juice in a food processor fitted with a metal blade until pureed. Press puree through a fine mesh strainer to remove seeds. Mix seedless puree with corn syrup and cooled sugar mixture in a bowl. Chill 1 hour.

Pour mixture into the freezer can of an ice cream maker and freeze about 30 minutes, or freeze according to manufacturer's instructions. Store leftovers in freezer.

Makes 5 cups.

FROZEN STRAWBERRY MARGARITA SQUARES

A pretty pink dessert easy to prepare for ahead of time…use a sharp knife dipped in hot water for easy cutting of any frozen dessert.

Crust
1¼ cups crushed pretzels
4 tablespoons butter, melted

Filling
1 14-ounce can sweetened condensed milk
1 cup pureed strawberries
½ cup fresh lime juice
1 8-ounce container frozen nondairy whipped topping, thawed

Topping
1 cup sliced strawberries

Crust: Mix pretzel crumbs and butter in a 13x9-inch baking pan. Press mixture firmly onto bottom of pan. Chill.

Filling: Mix sweetened condensed milk, strawberry puree and lime juice in a bowl until blended. Stir in whipped topping. Pour mixture into prepared crust. Freeze 6 hours. Let stand at room temperature 15 minutes before cutting.

Topping: Garnish with sliced strawberries when serving. Freeze leftovers.

Makes 16 servings.

FROZEN STRAWBERRY CREAM POPS

Kids will love 'em.
Variation: Stir ½ cup mini-chocolate chips into cheese mixture before freezing.

**1 pint fresh strawberries, hulled or 2 cups frozen unsweetened
  strawberries, thawed**

2 cups whole milk ricotta cheese
¼ cup granulated sugar, or to taste
1 tablespoon fresh lemon juice

Puree strawberries in a blender, food processor or an electric mixer.

Add cheese, sugar and lemon juice; blend or process 2 minutes. Pour mixture
into freezer pop molds or 3-ounce plastic coated cups. Cover with pop mold
tops or foil. Insert clean popsicle wooden sticks. Freeze until firm, about
3 hours. Freeze leftovers.

Makes 12 pops.

MANGO SORBET WITH STRAWBERRY DAIQUIRI SAUCE

Light and delicious.

2 cups fresh strawberries, hulled
½ cup powdered sugar
⅓ cup dark rum
¼ cup fresh lime juice

1½ cups mango sorbet
lime zest

Process all ingredients except mango sorbet and lime zest in a blender until smooth.

Scoop sorbet into 6 individual dessert dishes. Pour strawberry daiquiri mixture around the sorbet. Garnish with lime zest. Serve immediately.

Makes 6 servings.

MANGO SORBET WITH STRAWBERRY SAUCE

Homemade mango sorbet...so good.

Sauce
2 cups fresh strawberries
4 tablespoons granulated sugar
4 tablespoons orange-flavored liqueur or orange juice

Sorbet
4 ripe firm mangoes, peeled, pitted and cubed
⅔ cup granulated sugar
½ cup corn syrup
6 tablespoons fresh lemon juice

Sauce: Puree first three ingredients in a blender; pour into a glass bowl. Refrigerate until ready to use. Refrigerate leftovers.

Sorbet: Process all sorbet ingredients in a blender or food processor fitted with a metal blade. Pulse to chop then process until thick and smooth. Pour mixture into the can of an ice cream maker. Freeze according to the manufacturer's instructions. Store in freezer.

To serve, scoop sorbet into dessert dishes and top with strawberry sauce.

Makes about 5 cups or 8 servings.

NO-COOK STRAWBERRY ICE CREAM

Simple and delicious.

1 14-ounce can sweetened condensed milk
1 5-ounce can evaporated milk
2 tablespoons granulated sugar
1½ cups whole milk

1 16-ounce package unsweetened frozen strawberries, thawed
2 tablespoons fresh lemon juice
¼ teaspoon salt

Mix first four ingredients in a 2-quart pitcher or a large bowl until blended. Cover and place in freezer 30 minutes.

Process strawberries, lemon juice and salt with steel blade in food processor until smooth; stir mixture into milk mixture. Pour mixture into freezer container of an ice cream maker (at least 1-quart). Freeze according to manufacturer's instructions.

Remove container with ice cream from ice cream maker, and place in freezer 15 minutes. Then transfer ice cream to an airtight container and freeze until firm, about 1½ hours.

Makes about 1½ quarts.

RHUBARB-STRAWBERRY ICE CREAM

Rhubarb lovers…this one's for you!

3 cups sliced rhubarb, fresh or frozen, do not thaw if frozen
2 cups granulated sugar
2 cups cold water
1 cup fresh sliced strawberries
3 cups miniature marshmallows
3 tablespoons fresh lemon juice
2 cups whipping cream
red food color, optional

Mix rhubarb, sugar, water and strawberries in a 4-quart saucepan. Bring to a boil, then reduce heat and simmer uncovered, stirring occasionally, until rhubarb is very tender, about 15 minutes. Reduce heat. Add marshmallows and lemon juice; stir and cook until marshmallows are melted. Place mixture in a very large mixing bowl. Cover and refrigerate until completely chilled, at least 8 hours.

Beat whipping cream in a large chilled mixing bowl with an electric mixer until soft peaks form. Fold whipped cream into chilled rhubarb mixture. Stir in a drop or two of food color, if desired. Pour mixture into a 4 to 5-quart ice cream freezer, and freeze following the manufacturer's directions. Scoop ice cream into a freezer container. Cover and freeze about 4 hours or until firm. Store in freezer.

Makes about 10 cups.

STRAWBERRY CHEESECAKE ICE CREAM

An easy homemade dessert…no cooking required!

1 pint fresh strawberries, coarsely chopped
1 8-ounce package cream cheese, softened
1 cup granulated sugar
1 cup whole milk
1 tablespoon fresh lemon juice
1 teaspoon pure vanilla extract
⅛ teaspoon salt

½ cup heavy cream

Place all ingredients, except ½ cup heavy cream, in a blender. Process just until smooth.

Stir in heavy cream. Pour mixture into an ice cream maker, and freeze following manufacturer's directions. Spoon ice cream into airtight freezer containers and let harden in freezer. Store in freezer.

Makes 8 servings.

STRAWBERRY BUTTERMILK GELATO

Creamy gelato…a frosty treat.

2 cups granulated sugar
2 cups water
5 cups fresh strawberries, quartered
2 cups low-fat buttermilk

Mix sugar and water in a large saucepan. Bring mixture to a boil, stirring constantly until sugar is dissolved. Pour into a large bowl and cool completely.

Puree strawberries in a blender until smooth. Add puree and buttermilk to sugar syrup in bowl; stir until well mixed. Pour mixture into freezer can of an ice cream maker. Freeze according to the manufacturer's instructions. Serve or store in freezer.

Makes 8 cups.

STRAWBERRY DAIQUIRI FROZEN DESSERT

Pretty pink dessert…good one to prepare ahead of time.

1 3-ounce package ladyfingers, split in half lengthwise
2 tablespoons light rum or apricot nectar

1 8-ounce container frozen nondairy whipped topping,
thawed, divided
1 8-ounce package cream cheese, softened
1 16-ounce package frozen strawberries, thawed
1 10-ounce container frozen strawberry daiquiri mix, thawed

Place ladyfinger halves cut side up, in bottom of an 11x7-inch baking dish. Brush with rum or apricot nectar.

Reserve 1 cup whipped topping in a small bowl; refrigerate. Process cream cheese in a food processor until fluffy. Add remaining whipped topping, strawberries and daiquiri mix; process until blended. Pour mixture over ladyfingers. Freeze at least 6 hours. Let stand at room temperature 20 minutes before serving. Cut into squares. Garnish with reserved whipped topping. Freeze leftovers.

Makes 10 servings.

STRAWBERRY GRANITA

You don't need an ice cream maker to prepare this frosty dessert.

½ cup granulated sugar
½ cup warm water

3 cups sliced strawberries
2 tablespoons fresh lemon juice

Process sugar and water in a blender until sugar dissolves.

Add strawberries and lemon juice; process until smooth. Pour mixture into an 8-inch square baking dish. Cover and freeze 3 hours. Remove from freezer; stir well. Cover and freeze at least 5 hours.

Remove from freezer and let stand at room temperature 10 minutes. Scrape entire mixture with a fork until fluffy. Serve. Freeze leftovers.

Makes 4 cups.

STRAWBERRY ICE CREAM

Summer and a dish of this ice cream…can it get any better!

3 cups half and half

6 egg yolks
1 cup granulated sugar
pinch of salt

2 cups thinly sliced fresh strawberries, mashed
2 teaspoons pure vanilla extract

Heat half and half in a saucepan over medium heat 4 minutes.

Whisk egg yolks, sugar and salt in bowl until well blended. Gradually whisk in hot half and half until well blended. Pour mixture into another saucepan. Cook over medium-low heat, stirring constantly with a wooden spoon, until custard is thick enough to coat back of a metal spoon, about 8–10 minutes. Do not boil custard.

Pour custard through a fine-mesh sieve set over a clean bowl. Stir in strawberries and vanilla extract. Cool to room temperature, then refrigerate until cold.

Pour mixture into the freezer can of an ice cream maker. Freeze according to the manufacturer's instructions. Place ice cream into freezer containers; cover and freeze until firm before serving, about 3 hours. Freeze leftovers.

Makes about 1 quart.

STRAWBERRY ICE CREAM SANDWICHES

Homemade cookies hold this delicious ice cream sandwich.

1 cup brown sugar, packed
1 cup butter, softened
1½ cups mashed ripe bananas
2 eggs
1 teaspoon pure vanilla extract
2¼ cups all-purpose flour, mixed
   in a large bowl with 1¾ cups
   old-fashioned oats, uncooked
1 teaspoon baking soda

½ teaspoon salt
¼ teaspoon ground cinnamon

3 cups strawberry ice cream, softened
1½ cups semi-sweet chocolate chips,
   melted with 1 teaspoon solid
   shortening
½ cup finely chopped nuts, optional

Preheat oven to 350°.

Beat sugar and butter in a large mixer bowl until creamy. Beat in bananas, eggs and vanilla extract until well mixed. Add flour mixture; beat until well mixed. Drop dough by ¼-cupfuls 3 inches apart onto ungreased baking sheets. Flatten each to a 3-inch diameter with bottom of a glass dipped in granulated sugar. Bake until edges are lightly browned, 14–19 minutes. Remove from oven; let stand 2 minutes on baking sheet, then remove from baking sheet and cool completely on a wire rack. Freeze until firm, about 2 hours.

Spread ¼ cup ice cream over flat side of 1 cookie; top with another cookie flat side down. Press together slightly. Spread 1 tablespoon melted chocolate over top of each sandwich cookie. Sprinkle with nuts. Place sandwiches on an ungreased baking sheet; freeze 2 hours. When chocolate is set place sandwiches in a food plastic freezer bag. Store in freezer.

Makes 1 dozen.

142

STRAWBERRY MARGARITA FREEZE

Garnish this cool dessert with fresh strawberry halves when serving.

1½ cups crushed pretzels
¼ cup butter or margarine, melted

1 8-ounce package cream cheese, softened
½ cup granulated sugar
1⅓ cups fresh orange juice or thawed non-alcoholic strawberry margarita mix
1 cup crushed strawberries
1 8-ounce container frozen nondairy whipped topping, thawed

Crust: Mix pretzels and butter in a bowl; press mixture onto bottom of a 9-inch springform pan.

Beat cream cheese and sugar with an electric mixer on medium speed until well blended. Gradually beat in orange juice until well blended. Stir in crushed strawberries. Stir in whipped topping with a wire whisk until blended. Pour mixture over prepared crust. Freeze until firm. Let stand 15 minutes at room temperature before serving. Freeze leftovers.

Makes 16 servings.

STRAWBERRY SHERBET

Homemade sherbet…refreshing!

2 pints very ripe strawberries, stemmed
3 tablespoons fresh lemon juice
2 tablespoons light corn syrup
1 cup granulated sugar, or less depending on flavor of strawberries

Puree strawberries in food processor. Stir lemon juice and corn syrup. Gradually mix in sugar. Pour mixture into container of ice cream freezer. Freeze according to manufacturer's instructions. Place sherbet into a clean freezer container; cover and freeze 4 hours. Freeze leftovers.

Makes about 1 quart.

STRAWBERRY SNOW CONES

The kids are going to love them…save one for yourself!

1 package (8-serving size) strawberry flavor gelatin mix
1 cup boiling water
1 cup pureed strawberries
½ cup light corn syrup
½ cup ice cubes

8 cups crushed ice
8 8-ounce clean paper or plastic cups

Stir gelatin and boiling water in a large bowl until completely dissolved, about 2 minutes. Add strawberries, corn syrup and ice cubes; stir until blended and ice is completely melted.

Fill each cup with 1 cup of crushed ice. Pour gelatin mixture evenly over ice. Serve immediately.

For leftovers: Wrap filled cups well with plastic food wrap; store in freezer up to 3 weeks. Remove from freezer 5 minutes before serving.

Makes 8 servings.

STRAWBERRY-PINEAPPLE SORBET

Pineapple juice lends a little tang.

3 cups chopped fresh strawberries
¾ cup pineapple juice
½ large banana
¼ cup water

Puree all ingredients in a food processor or blender until smooth.

Press mixture with the back of a spoon through a fine sieve into a medium bowl; discard pulp in sieve. Cover; chill at least 6 hours.

Stir mixture and place into the freezer can of an ice cream maker. Freeze according to manufacturer's instructions. Store leftovers in freezer.

Makes 4 servings.

Jams
Conserve

MICROWAVE STRAWBERRY JAM

Frozen strawberries may be used; thaw, but do not drain.

1 cup mashed fresh strawberries
¾ cup granulated sugar
2 teaspoons fresh lemon juice
¼ teaspoon butter or margarine (to prevent excess foaming)

Mix all ingredients in a 2-quart microwave-safe casserole. Microwave on 100% power (high) for 8–9 minutes or until mixture thickens and is reduced to about 1 cup, stirring every 2 minutes. Cool. Cover and chill. The mixture will thicken as it cools. If too stiff, stir in 1 teaspoon water at a time to reach desired consistency. Refrigerate leftovers.

Makes about 1 cup.

STRAWBERRY-ORANGE FREEZER JAM

Frozen strawberries are used in this sweet jam.

**2 10-ounce packages frozen sweetened strawberries, thawed but
   not drained**
1 1¾-ounce package powdered fruit pectin
1 tablespoon freshly grated orange peel
½ cup fresh orange juice
3½ cups granulated sugar

Stir strawberries, fruit pectin, orange peel and orange juice in a 3-quart
saucepan until pectin is dissolved. Bring to a rolling boil over high heat, stirring
constantly. Stir in sugar. Heat to a rolling boil, stirring constantly.

Remove from heat and immediately skim off foam. Immediately pour jam
into hot, sterilized jars or freezer containers, leaving a ½-inch headspace.
Wipe rims of jars. Seal immediately. Cool on a rack. Refrigerate up to
1 week or freeze up to 3 months.

Makes 4 half pints.

STRAWBERRY-RHUBARB JAM

Share a pint.

1 16-ounce package frozen rhubarb, thawed
2 10-ounce packages frozen strawberries in syrup, thawed
½ cup cold water
1 package (1¾ ounce) powdered fruit pectin
½ teaspoon butter or margarine (to reduce foaming)
4½ cups granulated sugar

Sterilize canning jars, lids and bands according to manufacturer's directions. Always use new lids.

Chop rhubarb into small pieces; mix with strawberries in a bowl. Measure exactly 4 cups fruit and place into a 6 to 8-quart saucepot. Stir in ½ cup water, then stir in pectin. Add butter. Bring mixture to a full rolling boil. Stir in sugar. Return to a full boil. Boil exactly 1 minute, stirring constantly. Remove from heat. Skim off foam with a metal spoon. Ladle immediately into prepared jars, filling to within ⅛-inch of tops. Wipe jar rims and threads. Cover with two-piece lids. Screw bands tightly.

Fill boiling water canner half full with water. Place jars on a rack in center of the canner. Water must cover jars by 1–2 inches. Cover canner and bring water to a gentle boil.

Process in a boiling water bath 10 minutes. Remove jars and place upright on a clean kitchen towel to cool completely. After jars are cool, check seals by pressing middle of lid with your finger. If lid springs back, lid is not sealed, and refrigeration is necessary.

Makes about 3 pints.

RHUBARB-STRAWBERRY CONSERVE

Try this delicious spread on warm buttered biscuits for a special breakfast treat.

2 cups granulated sugar
½ cup water
4 cups fresh rhubarb cut in 1-inch pieces
2 cups fresh strawberries, halved
½ cup coarsely chopped walnuts
½ cup golden raisins

Bring sugar and water to a boil in a 3-quart saucepan, stirring constantly. Stir in rhubarb; cook on medium-low heat about 15 minutes, stirring often, until thickened.

Stir in strawberries, walnuts and raisins. Bring to a boil and cook on medium-low heat 5 minutes.

Remove from heat. Skim off foam immediately, and immediately pour conserve into hot sterilized jars, leaving a ¼-inch headspace. Wipe rims of jars, and seal. Cool on a rack 1 hour. Store in refrigerator up to 1 month.

Makes 4 half pints.

Meals
Paired with
Strawberries

CHOCOLATE WAFFLES WITH STRAWBERRIES AND CREAM

Kids will love 'em!

2 cups all-purpose flour
¼ cup granulated sugar
1½ teaspoons baking powder
½ teaspoon baking soda
¼ teaspoon salt

2 large eggs, separated
1 cup whole milk
¼ cup butter or margarine, melted
½ cup chocolate-flavored syrup
½ cup dairy sour cream

thinly sliced fresh strawberries
sweetened whipped cream or soft vanilla ice cream

Whisk flour, sugar, baking powder, baking soda and salt in a large mixing bowl until well blended. In another bowl, whisk egg yolks, milk and melted butter. Stir in chocolate-flavored syrup and sour cream; stir mixture into dry ingredients until well moistened. The batter will have some lumps; set aside.

Whip egg whites in another bowl to soft peaks; fold into batter. (Batter should be thick).

Preheat waffle iron. When hot, brush or spray the grids lightly with vegetable oil or as directed by the manufacturer. Pour batter into center of waffle iron; gently spread with a kitchen knife. Close waffle iron and cook 3–4 minutes or until steam escaping from sides is greatly reduced. Open waffle iron. If it sticks a little, the waffle is not yet done. Continue cooking for another minute. Remove waffle with tines of a fork. Repeat with remaining batter.

Serve immediately topped with sliced strawberries and a dollop of whipped cream or soft vanilla ice cream. Refrigerate leftovers.

Makes four 7-inch square waffles.

153

GRILLED CATFISH WITH STRAWBERRY SALSA

Almost gourmet…serve with hard rolls.

6 tablespoons butter
2 teaspoons Dijon type mustard
4 6-ounce catfish fillets

Salsa
2 cups ripe strawberries, hulled and chopped
2 tablespoons mint leaves, chopped
2 tablespoons granulated sugar
2 tablespoons dark rum
½ teaspoon freshly ground black pepper

Melt butter in a small saucepan over medium heat. Whisk in mustard.

Prepare a hot grill fire. When ready to grill, place an oiled grill rack over fire. Lightly baste each side of the fish with butter-mustard mixture. Place fish on rack. Grill until opaque and just beginning to flake (test with a fork), about 4–5 minutes per side, turning once and basting frequently with butter-mustard mixture. Serve with salsa. Refrigerate leftovers.

Salsa: Mix all salsa ingredients in a medium bowl. Serve chilled or at room temperature. Refrigerate leftovers.

Makes 4 servings.

GRILLED SALMON WITH STRAWBERRY SALSA

Variation: Use other firm fish fillets such as halibut.

Salsa
1 seedless cucumber, finely chopped
2 green onions, thinly sliced
1 tablespoon chopped cilantro
4 tablespoons rice wine vinegar
salt and pepper, adjusted to taste
2 cups fresh strawberries,
  coarsely chopped

Sauce
½ cup butter
2 cloves garlic, chopped
2 tablespoons soy sauce
1 tablespoon honey
1 tablespoon fresh lemon juice

6 skinless salmon fillets

Salsa: Mix all ingredients except strawberries in a glass bowl. Cover and refrigerate at least 1 hour, longer if possible. Stir in strawberries just before serving.

Sauce: Melt butter in a small saucepan over low heat until hot. Stir in garlic. Stir in soy sauce, honey and lemon juice; cook and stir 2 minutes.

Brush salmon with sauce and place on an oiled fish grilling rack. Place rack 4 inches from fire. Grill 4–5 minutes on each side, brushing with sauce while cooking. Serve immediately with salsa. Refrigerate leftovers.

Makes 6 servings.

OVERNIGHT FRENCH TOAST WITH STRAWBERRY SAUCE

Brunch becomes special with this delicious dish.

1 1-pound loaf Challah or French
   bread, cubed
1 8-ounce package cream cheese,
   cut into small pieces

1 pint fresh strawberries, sliced
1 10-ounce jar strawberry preserves

6 eggs
4 cups half and half (light cream)
½ cup butter or margarine, melted
¼ cup maple syrup
1 teaspoon pure vanilla extract

Lightly grease a 13x9-inch baking pan.

Place half the bread cubes into prepared pan. Sprinkle evenly with cheese.
Top with remaining bread cubes.

Whisk eggs, half and half, butter, syrup and vanilla extract in a large bowl
with a wire whisk until smooth. Pour mixture evenly over bread cubes;
press down lightly. Cover with aluminum cooking foil and immediately
refrigerate for at least 8 hours.

Preheat oven to 350°.

Bake covered 25 minutes. Uncover and continue baking 20 minutes.

Heat strawberries and preserves in a medium saucepan over low heat.
Spoon over freshly baked French toast. Refrigerate leftovers.

Makes 8 servings.

PANCAKES WITH FRESH STRAWBERRIES

You'll find a touch of lemon in these tasty pancakes. Substitute 3 cups frozen strawberries, thawed, if desired.

2⅓ cups all-purpose flour
⅓ cup powdered sugar
1½ teaspoons baking soda
1 teaspoon baking powder

1 cup whole milk
1 cup dairy sour cream
2 eggs

2 tablespoons butter, melted
2 tablespoons fresh lemon juice
1 tablespoon lemon zest

Topping
½ cup red currant jelly
3 cups fresh strawberries, halved

Pancakes: Mix flour, powdered sugar, baking soda and baking powder in a large bowl. Mix remaining pancake ingredients in another bowl until smooth; stir into flour mixture until well mixed (batter will be thick).

Heat a lightly greased griddle or frying pan to 350° or until a drop of water sizzles.

Spoon ¼ cup batter for each pancake onto hot griddle; spread to form a 4-inch circle. Cook until bubbles form on top, about 1–2 minutes. Turn pancakes and continue cooking until browned, about 1–2 minutes. Keep warm. Repeat with remaining batter.

Topping: Melt currant jelly in a 2-quart saucepan over medium heat. Remove from heat. Stir in strawberries until coated. Serve over warm pancakes. Refrigerate leftovers.

Makes 8 servings.

STRAWBERRIES AND CREAM PANCAKES

Serve with a side of crisp bacon.

3 cups fresh strawberries
¼ cup granulated sugar

2 cups all-purpose baking mix
2 tablespoons granulated sugar
1 cup whole milk
1 teaspoon pure vanilla extract
2 large eggs

1½ cups heavy whipping cream, whipped

Heat electric griddle to 375°. Or heat a standard griddle or skillet over medium-high heat; grease with cooking spray, corn oil or shortening.

Mix strawberries and ¼ cup sugar in a bowl; set aside.

Stir baking mix, 2 tablespoons sugar, milk, vanilla and eggs in a bowl until well blended. Pour mixture by scant ¼-cupfuls onto hot griddle or skillet. Cook until edges are dry. Turn pancakes and cook until golden.

Serve immediately, layering pancakes, strawberries and whipped cream. Drizzle with strawberry syrup as desired. Refrigerate leftovers.

Makes 4 servings.

TURKEY STRAWBERRY SANDWICH

Strawberries and turkey makes a very tasty sandwich.

4 slices whole wheat bread
2 lettuce leaves
2 slices Swiss cheese
¼ pound thinly sliced deli turkey breast
4 fresh strawberries, sliced

2 tablespoons whipped cream cheese spread mixed in a small bowl
  with 2 teaspoons finely chopped pecans

Layer lettuce, cheese, turkey and strawberries on two slices of bread.
Spread cream cheese mixture over other two slices of bread; place over
strawberries. Serve immediately.

Makes 2 servings.

Pies

BANANA-STRAWBERRY CREAM PIE

Homemade custard makes this pie special. Top with sweetened whipped cream when serving.

1 9-inch baked pie shell, cooled

Filling
½ cup granulated sugar
2 tablespoons cornstarch
¼ teaspoon salt
4 egg yolks
2 cups cold whole milk
1½ teaspoons pure vanilla extract

2 cups fresh strawberries, sliced, divided
2 small ripe bananas, sliced

Filling: Mix sugar, cornstarch and salt in a medium saucepan. Mix egg yolks and milk in a small bowl until blended; stir a small amount into sugar mixture until blended. Gradually stir in remaining egg mixture until well blended. Cook over medium heat, stirring constantly, until mixture boils and is thickened. Boil 1 minute. Remove from heat. Stir in vanilla extract. Cool.

Reserve ¼ cup sliced strawberries; set aside. Place remaining strawberries in prepared pie shell. Pour half the cooled custard over strawberries. Top with bananas. Cover with remaining custard. Refrigerate and chill well. When serving, top with reserved strawberries. Refrigerate leftovers.

Makes 6 servings.

BIG BOY STRAWBERRY PIE

A family restaurant's famous strawberry pie.

1 9-inch deep dish baked pie shell

1 cup granulated sugar
1 cup cold water
3 tablespoons cornstarch mixed in a small bowl
    until blended with 1/2 cup cold water
1 3-ounce package strawberry flavor gelatin
1 teaspoon pure vanilla extract

4 cups fresh strawberries, hulled
1 cup whipping cream whipped in a bowl with 2 tablespoons
    granulated sugar and 1/2 teaspoon pure vanilla extract

Mix sugar and 1 cup water in a saucepan; bring to a boil over medium heat. Stir in cornstarch mixture. Cook, stirring often, until clear and thickened. Stir in dry strawberry gelatin. Stir in 1 teaspoon vanilla extract. Remove from heat. Cool slightly.

Arrange strawberries in baked pie shell. Pour slightly cooled mixture over top. Refrigerate and chill before serving. Top with whipped cream when serving. Refrigerate leftovers.

Makes 8 servings.

BLACK BOTTOM STRAWBERRY CREAM PIE

Fudge and cream cheese in this luscious strawberry pie.

1 9-inch baked pie shell, baked in a 9-inch glass pie plate
⅔ cup hot fudge topping (not chocolate syrup)

1 8-ounce package cream cheese, softened
1 cup powdered sugar
2 cups strawberries, quartered
½ cup prepared strawberry pie glaze
½ cup whipping cream whipped with 1 tablespoon powdered sugar
    and ½ teaspoon pure vanilla extract

Cool baked pie shell on a wire rack. Spread bottom of shell with hot fudge topping. Refrigerate 1 hour.

Beat cream cheese and powdered sugar with an electric mixer in a bowl on medium speed until smooth. Spread mixture over fudge layer. Mix strawberries and strawberry glaze in a bowl; spoon over cream cheese layer. Refrigerate until firm, about 1 hour. Top with dollops of sweetened whipped cream when serving. Refrigerate leftovers.

Makes 8 servings.

CHOCOLATE-TOPPED
STRAWBERRIES AND CREAM PIE

Cream cheese and whipped cream under fresh strawberries drizzled with chocolate!

1 9-inch baked pie shell, cooled

Filling
1 8-ounce cream cheese, softened
⅓ cup granulated sugar
1 teaspoon pure vanilla extract
1 cup whipping cream
4 cups fresh strawberries

Topping
½ cup semi-sweet chocolate chips
1 tablespoon solid shortening

Filling: Beat cream cheese in a mixer bowl on medium speed until fluffy. Beat in sugar and vanilla extract until smooth. Beat whipping cream in another bowl on high speed until soft peaks form. Fold whipped cream into cream cheese mixture. Spoon mixture into prepared pie shell. Place strawberries, pointed side up, over mixture. Refrigerate.

Topping: Melt chocolate chips and shortening in saucepan over low heat, stirring constantly, until smooth. Drizzle over strawberries. Refrigerate and chill until set, about 1 hour. Refrigerate leftovers.

Makes 8 servings.

COCONUT-CRUSTED FROZEN FLUFFY STRAWBERRY PIE

Garnish this luscious pie with fresh strawberries when serving.

Crust
2½ cups flaked coconut, toasted
⅓ cup butter

Filling
1 3-ounce package cream cheese, softened
1 14-ounce can sweetened condensed milk
2½ cups fresh or frozen, thawed, unsweetened strawberries,
    mashed or pureed
3 tablespoons lemon juice
1 cup whipping cream, whipped with 1 tablespoon powdered sugar
    and ½ teaspoon pure vanilla extract

Crust: Mix toasted coconut and butter in a bowl; press mixture firmly onto bottom and up sides to rim of a 9-inch lightly buttered pie plate.

Filling: Beat cream cheese in a large bowl until fluffy. Gradually beat in sweetened condensed milk until smooth. Stir in pureed strawberries and lemon juice. Fold in whipped cream. Pour mixture into prepared crust. Freeze 4 hours or until firm. Freeze leftovers.

Makes 8 servings.

COCONUT STRAWBERRY PIE

Garnish with sliced strawberries when serving.

2½ cups sweetened flaked coconut
⅓ cup butter, melted

4 cups fresh strawberries, sliced
¾ cup granulated sugar
½ teaspoon pure vanilla extract

½ cup cold water
1 envelope unflavored gelatin
2 teaspoons fresh lemon juice

1 cup whipping cream, whipped
   with 2 tablespoons powdered
   sugar and ½ teaspoon pure
   vanilla extract

Preheat oven to 300°.

Mix coconut and butter in a bowl; press mixture on bottom and up sides of a greased 9-inch glass pie plate. Bake until lightly browned, about 25 minutes. Remove from oven; cool on a wire rack.

Mix strawberries sugar and vanilla in a large bowl; let stand 10 minutes.

Place water in a small saucepan; sprinkle top with gelatin, and let stand 1 minute, then stir and cook over medium heat until gelatin is dissolved. Stir in lemon juice. Stir mixture into strawberry mixture. Cool to room temperature. Fold in whipped cream. Pour mixture into prepared cooled crust. Refrigerate 4–5 hours before serving. Refrigerate leftovers.

Makes 6 servings.

CREAMY STRAWBERRY PIE

Ice cream, strawberries and strawberry gelatin in this cool pie. Garnish with fresh sliced strawberries when serving if desired.

1 9-inch baked pie shell, cooled

Filling
1 10-ounce package sweetened sliced strawberries, thawed
1 3-ounce package strawberry flavor gelatin mix
2 cups vanilla ice cream

Drain strawberries, reserve juice; set strawberries aside.

Add enough water to juice to measure 1 cup; bring to a boil in a large saucepan over medium heat. Remove from heat. Stir in gelatin until completely dissolved. Stir in ice cream until just blended. Refrigerate until slightly thickened, 5–10 minutes. Fold in drained strawberries. Spoon mixture into prepared crust. Refrigerate until firm, about 1 hour. Refrigerate leftovers.

Makes 6 servings.

EASY STRAWBERRY CREAM PIE

Instant pudding makes this strawberry pie a snap to prepare.

1 9-inch prepared graham cracker pie crust

1 package (4-serving size) vanilla flavor instant pudding and pie mix
1 cup dairy sour cream
¼ cup whole milk
2 teaspoons freshly grated orange rind
½ teaspoon pure vanilla extract

1 8-ounce container frozen non-dairy whipped topping, thawed, divided

2 cups fresh strawberries, hulled

Mix dry pudding mix, sour cream, milk, orange rind and vanilla extract in a large bowl until well blended.

Add 2 cups thawed whipped topping; beat with a wire whisk 2 minutes or until well blended. Spoon half the mixture into crust. Place strawberries stem side down into mixture then top with remaining pudding mixture. Refrigerate immediately and chill 3 hours before serving. Garnish with remaining whipped topping when serving. Refrigerate leftovers.

Makes 6 servings.

FRESH STRAWBERRY PIE

A shortbread cookie crust is used for this sweet pie.

Crust
2 cups crushed shortbread cookies
⅓ cup butter, melted

3 tablespoons cornstarch
½ teaspoon pure vanilla extract
¼ teaspoon salt

Filling
6 cups strawberries, hulled, divided
1 cup granulated sugar

1 cup sweetened whipped cream

Preheat oven to 350°.

Crust: Mix all crust ingredients in a bowl. Press mixture onto bottom and up sides of an ungreased 9-inch glass pie plate. Bake 7 minutes. Remove from oven; cool completely.

Filling: Mash 1 cup strawberries, and add water to equal 1⅓ cups. Mix sugar and cornstarch in a 2-quart saucepan. Stir in mashed strawberry mixture. Cook over medium heat, stirring constantly, until thickens and comes to a full boil, about 15 minutes. Boil 1 minute. Remove from heat. Stir in vanilla extract and salt. Cool 10 minutes.

Place remaining strawberries into crust. Pour cooked strawberry mixture over strawberries. Refrigerate until thickened, about 3 hours. Garnish with sweetened whipped cream. Refrigerate leftovers.

Makes 8 servings.

FROZEN STRAWBERRY MARGARITA PIE

A good dessert to make ahead...delicious and pretty too.

Crust
1 cup finely crushed pretzels
⅓ cup butter, melted
3 tablespoons granulated sugar

Filling
**3 cups fresh strawberries,
reserving 4 whole strawberries
for topping**
**1 6-ounce can frozen limeade
concentrate, slightly thawed**

**3 tablespoons tequila or fresh
orange juice**
1 tablespoon fresh orange juice
**1 quart vanilla ice cream, slightly
softened**

Topping
**1 cup frozen nondairy whipped
topping, thawed**
8 miniature pretzels
4 reserved strawberries, sliced

Preheat oven to 350°.
Lightly butter a 9-inch pie pan.

Crust: Mix all crust ingredients in a bowl; press mixture onto bottom and up sides of prepared pie pan. Bake until lightly browned, about 8 minutes. Remove from oven; cool completely.

Filling: Puree strawberries in a food processor. Add ice cream, limeade, tequila and orange juice. Process until well mixed. Spoon mixture into prepared cooled crust. Freeze until firm, about 4 hours. Freeze leftovers.

Topping: When serving, garnish with dollops of whipped topping, pretzels and strawberries

Makes 8 servings.

FROZEN STRAWBERRY YOGURT PIE

This is a good pie to make ahead of time.
Variation: Strawberry-flavored yogurt.

Crust
2 cups vanilla wafer cookie crumbs
¼ cup butter, melted

Filling
2 cups fresh strawberries, hulled
**   and thoroughly chopped**

⅓ cup granulated sugar
2 8-ounce containers vanilla yogurt

1 cup heavy whipping cream
2 tablespoons powdered sugar
1 teaspoon pure vanilla extract

Preheat oven to 300°.

Crust: Mix all crust ingredients in a bowl; press mixture evenly onto bottom and up sides of an ungreased 9-inch pie plate. Bake until lightly browned, about 15 minutes. Remove from oven; cool completely.

Filling: Mix chopped strawberries, granulated sugar and yogurt in a large bowl; set aside.

Beat whipping cream in a bowl with an electric mixer to soft peaks. Add powdered sugar and vanilla extract, and continue beating to stiff peaks. Fold mixture into strawberry mixture. Spoon mixture into prepared crust. Cover and freeze until firm, about 8 hours. Remove from freezer 30 minutes before serving. Freeze leftovers.

Makes 10 servings.

MERINGUE-TOPPED STRAWBERRY ICE CREAM PIE

A marshmallow creme meringue and strawberry puree tops this luscious ice cream pie.

1 9-inch baked pie shell, cooled

Filling
**3 cups strawberry ice cream,
   slightly softened**
**3 cups French vanilla ice cream,
   slightly softened**

3 egg whites
1 cup marshmallow creme

Topping
**1 10-ounce package sweetened
   frozen strawberries, thawed**

Filling: Spread strawberry ice cream in bottom of baked pie shell; freeze 1 hour. Spread French vanilla ice cream on top of strawberry ice cream; freeze 1 hour.

Preheat oven to 425°.

Filling: Beat egg whites in a mixer bowl on high speed to stiff peaks. Reduce speed to low. Gradually beat in marshmallow creme until smooth. Spread onto frozen pie, sealing to the edges of crust. Bake 3–5 minutes or until meringue is lightly browned. Immediately freeze until firm, about 6 hours. Top with strawberry puree when serving. Freeze leftovers.

Topping: Puree strawberries in a blender. Store in refrigerator.

Makes 8 servings.

172

MILK CHOCOLATE STRAWBERRY CREAM CHEESE PIE

Milk chocolate lovers…this one's for you.

Crust
1¼ cups graham cracker crumbs
5 tablespoons butter, melted
¼ cup granulated sugar

Filling
1 12-ounce package milk chocolate chips
2 8-ounce packages cream cheese, softened
1½ teaspoons pure vanilla extract

Topping
1 16-ounce package frozen sliced
   strawberries in syrup, thawed
1 tablespoon fresh lemon juice
1 tablespoon cornstarch
sweetened whipped cream

Crust: Mix all crust ingredients in a bowl. Press mixture firmly onto bottom and up sides of an ungreased 9-inch pie pan. Bake 6 minutes. Cool.

Filling: Melt chocolate in a double boiler over hot water; stir until smooth. Cool to room temperature. Beat cream cheese in a mixer bowl on medium speed until fluffy. Beat in cooled chocolate until well blended. Pour mixture into prepared crust. Refrigerate and chill until firm.

Topping: Heat strawberries, including juice, in a saucepan over low heat until warm. Stir lemon juice and cornstarch in a cup until smooth; stir mixture into strawberries. Cook and stir over medium heat until clear and thickened, about 4 minutes. Cool to room temperature. Spread mixture over filling. Refrigerate and chill. Garnish with whipped cream as desired when serving. Refrigerate leftovers.

Makes 8 servings.

NO-BAKE BLUEBERRY-STRAWBERRY CHEESECAKE PIE

Only the crust is baked. Garnish with whipped topping when serving.

Crust
1½ cups graham cracker crumbs
5 tablespoons butter or margarine, melted
3 tablespoons granulated sugar

Filling
1 8-ounce package cream cheese, softened
2 tablespoons granulated sugar

1 teaspoon pure vanilla extract
1 cup thawed frozen nondairy whipped topping
½ cup fresh blueberries
1½ cups fresh strawberries, halved

¾ cup boiling water
1 package 4-serving size strawberry flavor gelatin
½ cup ice cubes

Preheat oven to 350°.

Crust: Mix all crust ingredients in a bowl; press mixture onto bottom and up sides of a 9-inch pie plate. Bake 6 minutes. Cool.

Filling: Beat cream cheese with 2 tablespoons sugar in a bowl until blended. Add vanilla. Mix in 1 cup whipped topping. Spread mixture onto bottom of completely cooled crust. Arrange blueberries in a single layer in center of pie. Place strawberries around blueberries.

Stir boiling water into gelatin in a large bowl until dissolved, about 2 minutes. Stir in ice cubes until melted. Let stand 5 minutes. Spoon mixture over berries. Refrigerate until firm, about 3 hours. Refrigerate leftovers.

Makes 8 servings.

PEACH-STRAWBERRY PIE

Peaches, strawberries and cream cheese in this refrigerated pie.

Crust
1¼ cups graham cracker crumbs
6 tablespoons butter, melted
¼ cup granulated sugar

1 16-ounce can sliced peaches,
well drained and cut in half
3 cups sliced fresh strawberries
1 16-ounce container strawberry glaze

Filling
1 8-ounce package cream cheese, softened
¼ cup granulated sugar
1 tablespoon whole milk
1 teaspoon pure vanilla extract

Preheat oven to 375°.

Crust: Mix all crust ingredients in a bowl; press firmly onto bottom and up sides of an ungreased 9-inch pie plate. Bake 6 minutes. Cool completely.

Filling: Beat cream cheese in a mixer bowl on medium speed until fluffy. Beat in sugar, milk and vanilla extract until blended. Spoon mixture into prepared crust.

Place sliced peaches over cheese mixture. Mix strawberries and glaze in a bowl; spoon over peaches. Refrigerate and chill 4 hours before serving. Refrigerate leftovers.

Makes 8 servings.

REFRIGERATED STRAWBERRY-RHUBARB PIE

Another delicious way to use that backyard rhubarb!

1 9-inch baked pie shell, completely cooled

Filling
3 cups fresh strawberries, divided
2 cups diced fresh rhubarb
1 cup granulated sugar
3 tablespoons cornstarch
½ cup cold water
1 tablespoon fresh lemon juice
¼ teaspoon salt

1 cup heavy whipping cream
2 tablespoons granulated sugar
1 teaspoon pure vanilla extract

Filling: Mash half the strawberries in a saucepan. Add rhubarb and 1 cup sugar. Mix cornstarch, water, lemon juice, ½ teaspoon pure vanilla extract and salt in a small bowl until dissolved. Add to strawberry mixture in saucepan. Cook and stir over medium heat until rhubarb is tender and mixture is thickened. Pour mixture into prepared pie shell. Top with remaining strawberries. Cover and chill in refrigerator.

Beat whipping cream with 2 tablespoons sugar and 1 teaspoon vanilla extract in a mixer bowl to stiff peaks. Spoon over pie when serving. Refrigerate leftover pie and whipped cream.

Makes 6 servings.

STRAWBERRIES 'N CREAM BROWNIE MUD PIE

Drizzle with more chocolate fudge ice cream topping…of course.

Brownie Crust
½ cup granulated sugar
¼ cup butter, softened
1 1-ounce square unsweetened baking chocolate, melted
1 egg
1 teaspoon pure vanilla extract
½ cup all-purpose flour
¼ teaspoon baking powder
⅛ teaspoon salt

Filling
1 cup thick chocolate fudge ice cream topping (not chocolate syrup)
1 quart strawberry ice cream, slightly softened

Topping
nondairy whipped topping, thawed
strawberry slices, fresh or frozen

Preheat oven to 350°.
Grease a 9-inch pie plate.

Brownie Crust: Beat sugar and butter in a large bowl with an electric mixer on medium speed until creamy. Add chocolate, egg and vanilla extract; beat until well mixed. Reduce speed to low. Add flour, baking powder and salt; beat until well mixed. Spread batter into prepared pie plate. Bake 15–18 minutes or until edges just begin to pull away from sides. Do not over bake. Remove from oven. Cool 1 hour.

Filling: Spread fudge ice cream topping over cooled brownie crust. Spread ice cream over topping. Cover and freeze until firm, about 4 hours.

Topping: Garnish each serving with whipped topping and strawberry slices. Freeze leftovers.

Makes 12 servings.

STRAWBERRY DAIQUIRI PIE

Garnish this tasty pie with sliced fresh strawberries.

Crust
1¼ cups graham cracker crumbs
6 tablespoons butter, melted
¼ cup granulated sugar

Filling
1 8-ounce package cream cheese, softened
1 14-ounce can sweetened condensed milk
⅔ cup frozen strawberry daiquiri mix, thawed
2 tablespoons light rum or 1 teaspoon rum extract
2 drops red food coloring, optional
1 cup whipping cream whipped in a mixer bowl with 2 tablespoons
powdered sugar and ½ teaspoon pure vanilla extract

Preheat oven to 375°.

Crust: Mix all crust ingredients in a bowl; press mixture firmly onto bottom and up sides of an ungreased 9-inch pie pan. Bake 6 minutes. Remove from oven; cool completely.

Filling: Beat cream cheese in a large mixer bowl until fluffy. Gradually beat in sweetened condensed milk until smooth. Stir in daiquiri mix, rum, and food coloring. Fold whipped cream. Pour mixture into prepared crust. Chill or freeze until firm, about 4 hours. Refrigerate or freeze leftovers.

Makes 6 servings.

STRAWBERRY MERINGUE PIE

Marshmallows in the filling…cracker crumbs and pecans in the meringue crust. A special pie indeed!

3 egg whites
¼ teaspoon cream of tartar
1 cup granulated sugar
½ cup crushed saltine cracker crumbs
½ cup chopped pecans
1 teaspoon pure vanilla extract

2 pints fresh strawberries
4 cups miniature marshmallows
1 8-ounce container frozen nondairy whipped topping, thawed

Preheat oven to 350°.
Grease a 10-inch deep-dish pie plate.

Beat egg whites and cream of tartar in a mixer bowl to soft peaks. Gradually beat in granulated sugar on high speed until stiff glossy peaks are formed. Fold in crackers crumbs, pecans and vanilla extract. Spread mixture onto bottom and up sides of prepared pie plate. Bake until lightly browned, about 25 minutes. Remove from oven; cool on a wire rack.

In a bowl, mash 1 pint strawberries; drain and reserve ½ cup juice. Set mashed strawberries aside. In a saucepan, over low heat, cook and stir ½ cup juice and marshmallows until marshmallows are melted; refrigerate until partially set, then fold into mashed strawberries. Fold in whipped topping. Slice remaining 1 pint strawberries; fold into mashed strawberry mixture. Spoon mixture into meringue crust. Refrigerate until set, about 3 hours. Refrigerate leftovers.

Makes 8 servings.

STRAWBERRY-RHUBARB PIE

Serve at room temperature…with vanilla ice cream, of course!

9-inch unbaked double pie crust

Filling
1 cup granulated sugar
2 tablespoons cornstarch
2 tablespoons quick-cooking tapioca
½ teaspoon ground cinnamon
⅛ teaspoon salt

3 cups strawberries, hulled and quartered lengthwise
3 cups fresh rhubarb cut into ½-inch pieces
1 teaspoon pure vanilla extract
1 tablespoon butter, cut up

Preheat oven to 350°.
Line bottom crust into a 9-inch glass pie plate; set aside.

Filling: Mix first five ingredients in a large bowl until blended.

Add strawberries, rhubarb and vanilla; toss gently until coated. Spoon mixture into prepared crust. Dot with butter. Top with remaining crust. Fold edge of top crust under the edge of bottom crust; crimp edges to seal. Cut several slits on top crust to allow steam to escape.

Bake about 50–60 minutes or until filling is thick and bubbling. Remove from oven. Cool on a wire rack until set. Refrigerate leftovers.

Makes 8 Servings.

STRAWBERRY-SWIRLED ICE CREAM PIE

Chocolate crusted pie with pureed strawberries in vanilla ice cream and more fresh strawberries on top!

Crust
1 9-ounce box thin chocolate wafers, finely crushed
1 tablespoon granulated sugar
¼ teaspoon ground cinnamon
½ cup butter, melted

Filling
2 pints vanilla ice cream, softened
1 quart fresh strawberries, pureed in a food processor with 1/4 cup strawberry jam, then strained, divided

Topping
3 cups fresh strawberries
remaining strawberry puree

Preheat oven to 350°.

Crust: Mix all crust ingredients in a bowl. Press mixture onto bottom and up sides of an ungreased 9-inch pie plate. Bake 8 minutes. Remove from oven. Cool completely.

Place ice cream in a large bowl. Swirl in 1½ cups strawberry puree. Spoon mixture into prepared cooled crust. Cover and freeze until solid.

Remove from freezer 30 minutes before serving. Top with 3 cups fresh strawberries and garnish with strawberry puree. Freeze leftovers.

Makes 8 servings.

STRAWBERRY TURNOVER PIES

A good snack to bring along on picnics.

Filling
1½ cups fresh strawberries, quartered
2 tablespoons granulated sugar
1 tablespoon cornstarch
½ teaspoon pure vanilla extract

Topping
1 egg beaten in a small bowl
granulated sugar

Crust
1¼ cups all-purpose flour
½ teaspoon salt
½ teaspoon granulated sugar
½ cup cold butter, cut into small pieces
3 tablespoons ice cold water (approximately)

Preheat oven to 425°.
Line a baking sheet with parchment paper.

Filling: Mix all filling ingredients in a bowl; set aside.

Crust: Mix flour, salt and sugar in a bowl until blended. Cut in butter with a pastry blender until mixture resembles coarse meal. Add water, a little at a time, and mix until dough forms. Add more water, a little at a time, if dough is crumbly. Form dough into a ball, then flatten into a disc. Wrap in food plastic wrap; chill 1 hour.

Roll dough out on a floured surface into a large rectangle ⅛-inch thick. Cut 6 rounds out with a 5-inch cookie cutter. Place on prepare baking sheet. Spoon about 2 tablespoons strawberry mixture onto half of each round. Fold dough over to cover strawberry mixture. Press edges to seal.

Topping: Brush tops of each pie with egg. Make a slit in top of each pie. Sprinkle with sugar. Bake until golden brown, about 20–25 minutes. Remove from oven; cool slightly before serving. Refrigerate leftovers.

Makes 6 turnovers.

VANILLA YOGURT STRAWBERRY PIE

A delicious no-bake pie.

Crust
**14 peanut butter sandwich cookies (shaped like a peanut),
   finely crushed**
3 tablespoons butter, melted

Filling
**2 10-ounce packages frozen sweetened sliced strawberries,
   finely chopped**
4 cups frozen vanilla yogurt (1 quart)
2 peanut butter sandwich cookies, crumbled

Crust: Mix all crust ingredients in a bowl. Press mixture firmly onto bottom and up side of a 9-inch buttered glass pie plate.

Filling: Spread half of chopped strawberries into crust. Spread with yogurt. Top with remaining chopped strawberries. Sprinkle with crumbled cookies. Freeze 3 hours before serving. If frozen for a longer period, let stand at room temperature 15 minutes. Freeze leftovers.

Makes 8 servings.

Salads
Soups

CRANBERRY-STRAWBERRY GELATIN SALAD

Strawberries, cranberries and cream cheese in this gelatin salad.

1 6-ounce package strawberry flavor gelatin
1 cup boiling water
1 16-ounce can whole-berry cranberry sauce
1 16-ounce package frozen strawberries
½ cup finely diced celery
¼ cup finely chopped nuts
1 8-ounce package cream cheese softened and cut into small
  pieces

sweetened whipped cream or thawed nondairy whipped topping

In a bowl, stir gelatin with boiling water until completely dissolved.
Refrigerate until slightly chilled. Stir in remaining ingredients. Pour mixture
into an 8-inch square baking dish. Garnish with whipped cream as desired.
Store in refrigerator.

Makes 8 servings.

FRESH STRAWBERRY-MANDARIN GELATIN MOLD

A fat-free, sugar-free salad…delicious.

1 8-serving size package orange flavor sugar-free gelatin
1½ cups boiling water
2 cups cold club soda

1 11-ounce can mandarin orange segments, drained
1 cup sliced fresh strawberries

Place gelatin in a large bowl. Stir in boiling water until gelatin is completely dissolved. Stir in club soda. Refrigerate until thickened, about 1½ hours.

Stir in orange segments and strawberries. Pour mixture into a 6-cup mold sprayed with cooking spray. Refrigerate until firm, about 4 hours.

To unmold, dip mold in warm water about 20 seconds. Gently pull gelatin from around edge with moist fingers. Place a moistened plate on top of mold. Invert plate and mold, hold mold and plate together and shake slightly to loosen. Remove mold. Store in refrigerator.

Makes 12 servings.

ORANGE-STRAWBERRY SALAD

Sour cream adds a little tang to this refreshing salad.

2 3-ounce packages strawberry flavor gelatin
2 cups boiling water
1 10-ounce package frozen sweetened strawberries, thawed, juice
reserved
⅓ cup orange juice
1 11-ounce can mandarin orange segments, drained

⅓ cup dairy sour cream mixed in a small bowl with 1 tablespoon
reserved mixture. Refrigerate.

Place gelatin in a large bowl. Add boiling water; stir until gelatin is completely dissolved. Stir in reserved strawberry juice and orange juice to gelatin mixture. Reserve 1 tablespoon mixture; set aside.

Cover and refrigerate remaining gelatin mixture until slightly thickened, about 1 hour. Stir in strawberries and orange segments. Pour into a 6-cup mold coated with non-stick cooking spray or a 9-inch glass baking dish. Cover and refrigerate until set, about 4 hours.

Serve salad topped with sour cream mixture. Refrigerate leftovers.

Makes 8 servings.

PINEAPPLE-STRAWBERRY SALAD

A quick salad to prepare. Top with whipped cream when serving.

1 6-ounce package strawberry flavor gelatin
1 cup boiling water
2 10-ounce packages frozen sweetened strawberries, thawed
2 8-ounce cans unsweetened crushed pineapple, drained
3 bananas, mashed

Place gelatin in a large bowl. Add boiling water; stir until gelatin is completely dissolved. Stir in remaining ingredients. Pour mixture into a 2-quart glass bowl. Refrigerate until firm.

Makes 8 servings.

STRAWBERRY PRETZEL SALAD

This is a delicious salad...could be a dessert, you decide.
Variation: For topping: Stir 1 16-ounce container dairy sour cream with ¼ cup granulated sugar in a bowl. Spread over strawberry layer and sprinkle with ¼ cup toasted chopped pecans.

Crust
2 cups crushed pretzels
¾ butter cup butter, melted
3 tablespoons granulated sugar

Filling
¾ cup granulated sugar
1 8-ounce package cream cheese, softened

Topping
additional whipped topping or whipped cream

1 teaspoon pure vanilla extract
1 8-ounce container frozen nondairy whipped topping, thawed

1 6-ounce package strawberry flavor gelatin
2 cups boiling water
2 10-ounce packages frozen strawberries in light syrup, thawed

Preheat oven to 400°.
Spray a 13x9-inch baking pan with cooking spray.

Crust: Mix all crust ingredients in a bowl. Press mixture firmly on bottom of prepared pan. Bake 7 minutes. Cool completely in pan.

Filling: Beat cream cheese, ¾ cup sugar and vanilla extract in a mixer bowl on medium speed until well blended. Fold in whipped topping. Spread mixture over cooled crust. Refrigerate until chilled.

Place gelatin in a bowl. Add boiling water and stir until gelatin is completely dissolved. Stir in strawberries. Spread mixture over cheese layer. Refrigerate; chill until set, about 8 hours. Serve with thawed whipped topping or sweetened whipped cream. Refrigerate leftovers.

Makes 10 servings.

STRAWBERRY MOLD

More than just strawberries in this delicious mold!

2 3-ounce packages strawberry flavor gelatin
1 cup boiling water
2 10-ounce containers frozen sliced strawberries
1 cup chopped pecans
3 medium size bananas, sliced
1 cup crushed pineapple, drained
1 cup dairy sour cream

Place gelatin in a large bowl. Add boiling water and stir until gelatin is dissolved. Stir in remaining ingredients except dairy sour cream.

Pour half the mixture into a salad mold. Refrigerate and chill until firm. Top evenly with dairy sour cream. Then top with remaining gelatin mixture. Refrigerate until firm. Refrigerate leftovers.

Makes 12 servings.

ASPARAGUS-SPINACH SALAD WITH STRAWBERRY DRESSING

A strawberry dressing tops this tasty salad.

Strawberry Dressing
½ cup fresh orange juice
2 tablespoons raspberry vinegar
2 tablespoons extra virgin olive oil
4 teaspoons honey
¼ teaspoon salt
1 cup fresh strawberries, hulled

Salad
1 pound tender asparagus spears, blanched and drained
8 cups trimmed spinach leaves
4 tablespoons toasted slivered almonds
fresh strawberries, hulled

Strawberry Dressing: Process orange juice, vinegar, olive oil, honey and salt in a food processor or blender until blended. Add strawberries; pulse on and off just until combined, do not puree, dressing should be chunky. Pour dressing into a glass container; cover and refrigerate.

Salad: Arrange 2 cups spinach on four salad plates. Top each with equal portions of asparagus. Drizzle with ⅓ cup strawberry dressing. Top each with 1 tablespoon toasted almonds. Garnish with fresh strawberries.

Makes 4 servings.

ASPARAGUS-STRAWBERRY CHICKEN SALAD

Grilled chicken is perfect for this salad. Serve with poppy seed muffins, crisp bread sticks or hard rolls.

1 pound fresh asparagus, trimmed and cut into 1-inch pieces
1 tablespoon extra virgin olive oil
¼ teaspoon salt
¼ teaspoon freshly ground pepper

8 cups spring mix salad greens
3 cups sliced fresh strawberries
½ small red onion, thinly sliced
½ cup toasted chopped walnuts

2 tablespoons balsamic vinegar
2 teaspoons granulated sugar
2 tablespoons extra virgin olive oil

2 fully cooked, grilled boneless, skinless chicken breast cut into thin strips

Preheat oven to 400°.

Mix asparagus with 1 tablespoon olive oil in a bowl. Place in a single layer onto a large baking pan. Sprinkle with salt and pepper. Bake until tender, about 15–20 minutes.

Mix salad greens, strawberries, onion, walnuts, asparagus and chicken in a large salad bowl. Whisk vinegar, sugar and 2 tablespoons olive oil in a small bowl. Pour over salad; toss to coat. Serve. Refrigerate leftovers.

Makes 6 servings.

CARROT-ASPARAGUS-STRAWBERRY SALAD WITH CHEESE

A balsamic dressing makes this salad special.

Salad
2 cups thinly sliced fresh carrots
½ pound asparagus spears,
cut into bite-size pieces

8 cups mixed salad greens
2 cups sliced fresh strawberries
½ cup balsamic vinaigrette
4 ounces crumbled goat or feta cheese
½ cup toasted pecan halves

Balsamic vinaigrette
½ cup extra virgin olive oil
½ cup white balsamic vinegar
1 clove crushed garlic
½ teaspoon ground mustard
1 teaspoon brown sugar
salt and pepper to taste

Salad: Place carrots and asparagus in a large saucepan of boiling water. Boil about 2 minutes or until color has brightened. Drain and immediately place into a bowl of ice water. Drain and pat dry. Place in a large bowl.

Add salad greens and strawberries. Add ½ cup vinaigrette; toss well and serve. Top with cheese and pecans. Refrigerate leftovers.

Balsamic vinaigrette: Whisk all vinaigrette ingredients in a small bowl until blended. Refrigerate leftovers.

Makes 4 servings.

GOUDA AND STRAWBERRY SALAD

Cheese and juicy strawberries topped with a strawberry dressing.

Salad
6 cups romaine lettuce or radicchio greens
8-ounces sliced Gouda cheese, cut into wedges
1½ cups sliced ripe juicy strawberries
½ cup toasted ground pecans

Strawberry vinaigrette
¼ cup seedless strawberry jam or preserves
¾ cup extra virgin olive oil
¾ cup red wine or strawberry vinegar
salt and pepper to taste

Salad: Arrange lettuce on four salad plates. Place evenly divided portions of cheese wedges and strawberries alternately on lettuce. Divide vinaigrette between four plates; top each with 2 tablespoons pecans.

Strawberry vinaigrette: Whisk all vinaigrette ingredients in a small bowl. Pour into a jar; cover and chill until ready to use.

Makes 4 servings.

HAM CHEESE FRESH STRAWBERRY SALAD

A perfect summer salad…serve with freshly baked hard rolls.

Salad
1½ cups cubed cooked ham, chicken or turkey
1 cup deli Swiss cheese, shredded
1 pint fresh strawberries, sliced
2 nectarines or peaches, peeled and sliced
6 cups mixed salad greens

Dressing
¼ cup orange juice
2 tablespoons vegetable oil
1 tablespoon white wine vinegar
½ teaspoon poppy seed
¼ teaspoon salt

Salad: Mix all salad ingredients in a serving bowl.

Dressing: Whisk all dressing ingredients in a small bowl. Pour dressing over salad; toss to coat. Refrigerate leftovers.

Makes 4 servings.

MOOSE'S STRAWBERRY SALAD

A nice salad to serve with cold sandwiches…so easy to prepare.

4 cups fresh strawberries (1 quart), rinsed and halved
1 20-ounce can pineapple chunks, drained
4 bananas, sliced

1 16-ounce container prepared strawberry glaze, chilled
   (usually found in the produce section by the strawberries)

Mix strawberries, pineapple and bananas in a glass bowl. Gently fold in strawberry glaze. Chill 30 minutes. Refrigerate leftovers.

Makes 6 servings.

PINEAPPLE-STRAWBERRY
FRESH FRUIT SALAD

Poppy seed dressing over fresh fruit...pure bliss.

Dressing
¼ **teaspoon freshly grated orange peel**
1 **tablespoon fresh orange juice**
⅓ **cup dairy sour cream**
1½ **teaspoons granulated sugar**
½ **teaspoon poppy seed**

Salad
2 **cups fresh pineapple chunks**
½ **cup quartered fresh strawberries**
½ **cup kiwi fruit pieces**
½ **cup fresh raspberries**
½ **cup cubed cantaloupe melon**

Dressing: Mix all dressing ingredients in a small bowl; cover and refrigerate.

Salad: When serving, mix all salad ingredients in a medium glass serving bowl. Add dressing and toss lightly. Refrigerate leftovers.

Makes 6 servings.

SPINACH AND STRAWBERRY SALAD

Fresh strawberries and spinach...good.

Salad
2 bunches baby spinach, rinsed and torn into bite-size pieces
4 cups sliced fresh strawberries

Dressing
½ cup vegetable oil
¼ cup white wine vinegar
½ cup granulated sugar
¼ teaspoon paprika
2 tablespoons sesame seeds
1 tablespoon poppy seeds

Salad: Toss spinach and strawberries in a large salad bowl.

Dressing: Whisk all dressing ingredients in a medium bowl until blended.
Pour mixture over salad; toss to coat.

Makes 8 servings.

STRAWBERRY BLEU CHEESE SALAD

Toasted pecans and red onion in this delicious salad.

Dressing
3 tablespoons raspberry vinegar
3 tablespoons balsamic vinegar
3 tablespoons extra virgin olive oil

½ cup chopped pecans, toasted
6 cups mixed salad greens
2 cups diced fresh strawberries
8 ounces crumbled bleu cheese
½ cup diced red onion

Dressing: Mix all dressing ingredients in a bowl until blended.

Mix remaining ingredients in a large salad bowl. Add salad dressing; toss. Serve. Refrigerate leftovers.

Makes 6 servings.

STRAWBERRY-LAYERED FRUIT SALAD

Key lime yogurt gives this fruit salad a special flavor.

1 20-ounce can pineapple chunks, well drained
1 cup fresh strawberry halves
2 cups green grapes
1 cup fresh blueberries
2 cups cubed ripe cantaloupe melon

1 6-ounce container key lime pie yogurt mixed in a small bowl with
   2 tablespoons fresh orange juice
½ cup toasted coconut

Layer fruit in a large glass-serving bowl in order listed. Pour yogurt mixture over fruit. Top with toasted coconut. Serve. Refrigerate leftovers.

Makes 8 servings.

SUMMER TOSSED STRAWBERRY SALAD

My good friend, Pamela Johnson, from Minnesota, shares this tasty strawberry salad recipe. Serve with warm rolls or poppy seed muffins.

1 head romaine lettuce, torn into bite-size pieces
1 red onion, thinly sliced
1 package slivered almonds, (stir-fry in 2 tablespoons granulated sugar over medium-high heat until sugar is crystallized, then cooled)
3 cups fresh strawberries, quartered

Dressing
¾ cup mayonnaise
½ cup granulated sugar
½ cup whole milk
2 tablespoons poppy seeds
2 tablespoons raspberry vinegar

Salad: Mix all salad ingredients in a large salad bowl.

Dressing: Mix all dressing ingredients in a bowl until blended. Pour over salad. Toss lightly and serve immediately. Refrigerate leftovers.

Makes 6 servings.

RHUBARB-STRAWBERRY SOUP

Substitution: Use 2 cups frozen strawberries, thawed with juice.

3 stalks fresh rhubarb cut into 1½-inch chunks (about 2 cups)
1 pint fresh strawberries, sliced
¼ cup fresh orange juice
5 tablespoons granulated sugar
½ cup dairy sour cream

Place rhubarb in a small microwave-safe dish; cover with food plastic wrap. Microwave on high 5 minutes or until tender. (Or cook in a small saucepan over medium heat until tender.) Cool slightly and place in a food processor. Add strawberries, orange juice, sugar and sour cream; process until smooth. Serve in small bowls. Refrigerate leftovers.

Makes 4 servings.

STRAWBERRY SOUP WITH CINNAMON CROUTONS

No, soup is not always hot…try this one, it's delicious.

Soup
1 quart fresh strawberries, hulled and halved
2 cups apple juice
1 cup dairy sour cream
½ cup brown sugar, packed
½ cup honey
2 tablespoons fresh lemon juice

1½ cups half and half (light cream)
3 tablespoons fresh lemon juice

Croutons
3 slices white bread, remove crust, cube bread
2 tablespoons butter
**½ teaspoon ground cinnamon mixed with ½ teaspoon granulated
  sugar**

Soup: Mix first six ingredients in a bowl; process half of mixture at a time in a blender until pureed. Place into a large bowl. Stir in cream and orange juice. Cover and refrigerate 2 hours before serving. Refrigerate leftovers.

Croutons: Saute bread cubes in butter over medium heat in a skillet until golden brown. Remove from heat. Sprinkle with cinnamon-sugar mixture; toss to coat. Cool. Stir soup when serving. Garnish with croutons.

Makes 6 servings.

Sauces
Syrups
Condiments

CREAMY STRAWBERRY SAUCE

Spoon over angel food cake and fresh strawberries.

2 cups fresh ripe strawberries, hulled
6 tablespoons light corn syrup
3 tablespoons strawberry liqueur

8 ounces mascarpone cheese
½ teaspoon pure vanilla extract

Process strawberries, corn syrup and liqueur in food processor or blender until pureed. Add mascarpone and vanilla extract; process until blended. Spoon into a covered container; chill several hours. Refrigerate leftovers.

Makes 2 cups.

QUICK STRAWBERRY SAUCE

A saucy topping for ice cream or pound cake.

1 16-ounce package frozen strawberries in syrup, thawed
½ cup orange juice
1 tablespoon cornstarch

Process strawberries and orange juice in food processor or blender until smooth. Pour mixture in a small saucepan. Stir in cornstarch until blended. Cook on medium-high heat until thickened, stirring occasionally. Cool completely. Refrigerate leftovers.

Makes 1¾ cups.

STRAWBERRY DESSERT SAUCE

A good sauce to use on pound cake, ice cream, cheesecake, etc.
Substitution: 2 cups frozen unsweetened strawberries, thawed.

3 tablespoons granulated sugar
1 tablespoon cornstarch
¼ cup cold water
2 cups fresh strawberries, mashed
1 tablespoon lemon juice

Mix sugar, cornstarch and water in a saucepan until smooth. Bring to a boil;
cook and stir 2 minutes or until thickened. Stir in strawberries. Stir in lemon
juice. Pour sauce into a small glass serving pitcher. Cover and refrigerate
until chilled. Refrigerate leftovers.

Makes 4 servings.

RHUBARB-STRAWBERRY SYRUP

Good served on ice cream, yogurt, French toast, etc.

¾ cup fresh rhubarb, trimmed and chopped
½ cup fresh strawberries, sliced
⅔ cup granulated sugar
½ cup water

Mix rhubarb, strawberries, sugar and water in a medium saucepan. Bring to a boil over medium-high heat. Cook and stir until rhubarb is very soft, about 15 minutes. Strain into a serving dish; discard pulp. Serve or store in an airtight container in the refrigerator up to 4 days.

Makes 1¼ cups.

FRESH STRAWBERRY SYRUP

Great on French toast.

1 quart fresh strawberries, hulled and sliced
½ cup granulated sugar
¼ cup fresh orange juice
1 teaspoon grated fresh orange rind

Mix all ingredients in a medium saucepan; let stand 30 minutes or until sugar is dissolved. Cover over low heat, stirring occasionally, about 5 minutes or until warm. Pour into a serving pitcher. Refrigerate leftovers.

Makes 2 cups.

FRESH OR FROZEN STRAWBERRY SYRUP

A special syrup for those pancakes or waffles.

Fresh
1 pint fresh strawberries, hulled and halved
1 cup granulated sugar
¾ cup light corn syrup

Cook strawberries in a 3-quart saucepan over medium heat, stirring occasionally, until strawberries come to a full boil, about 6–8 minutes.

Line a strainer with cheesecloth; place over a bowl. Pour hot strawberries into strainer, mashing with back of a spoon to extract juice; discard pulp. Pour juice into saucepan. Stir in sugar and corn syrup. Cook over medium heat until mixture comes to a full boil, about 9 minutes. Boil 1 minute. Skim foam; and cool slightly. Store in a glass container in the refrigerator.

Frozen
Use one 16-ounce bag frozen strawberries instead of fresh strawberries. Increase cooking time of strawberries to 15 minutes, then follow fresh instructions. Refrigerate.

Makes 2 cups.

STRAWBERRY BALSAMIC VINAIGRETTE

Substitution: Dark balsamic vinegar may be used.

1½ cups strawberry preserves
¼ cup white balsamic vinegar
¼ cup olive oil
¼ teaspoon crushed rosemary
¼ teaspoon salt
¼ teaspoon ground white pepper

Process all ingredients in a blender until smooth. Spoon into a covered glass container. Refrigerate leftovers.

Makes about 2 cups.

STRAWBERRY CHUTNEY

A little chutney goes a long way…serve with ham or turkey.

¼ **cup brown sugar, packed**
¼ **cup fresh lemon juice**
¼ **cup raspberry vinegar**
2 **tablespoons raisins**
2 **tablespoons honey**
¼ **teaspoon freshly grated orange peel**
¼ **teaspoon prepared mustard**

2 **cups sliced fresh strawberries**

Mix first seven ingredients in a saucepan. Bring to a boil. Reduce heat to medium and cook uncovered 15 minutes or until slightly thickened, stirring occasionally.

Stir in strawberries. Pour mixture into a glass bowl; cover and refrigerate 8 hours. Refrigerate leftovers.

Makes 9 servings.

STRAWBERRY SALSA

Use it as a dip, or to accompany grilled seafood or chicken, etc.

1 jalapeno pepper, seeded and minced
½ medium red onion, thinly sliced
½ each red bell pepper, yellow bell pepper, green bell pepper,
   seeded and cut into thin strips
¼ cup finely shredded fresh cilantro leaves
1 cup fresh strawberries, sliced
¼ cup fresh orange juice
2 tablespoons fresh lime juice
2 tablespoons extra virgin olive oil
salt and freshly ground black pepper to taste

Toss all ingredients in a large glass bowl. Cover and refrigerate 3 hours.
Remove salsa from refrigerator just before serving. Refrigerate leftovers.

Makes about 2½ cups.

STRAWBERRY VINEGAR

A good vinegar to use in salad dressings or marinades.

1 pint fresh strawberries, sliced
2 cups white wine vinegar
2 tablespoons granulated sugar

Mix all ingredients in a glass bowl. Cover and let stand at room temperature for 2 days. Discard strawberries with a slotted spoon. Strain vinegar through a fine sieve lined with a triple thickness of rinsed and squeezed clean cheesecloth into a bowl. Pour vinegar in a sterilized glass jar with a lid. Refrigerate.

Makes 2 cups.

Shortcakes
Coffeecakes
Cupcakes

CLASSIC STRAWBERRY SHORTCAKE

Strawberry shortcake...an all-time favorite.

4 cups fresh strawberries, sliced
⅔ cup granulated sugar, or to taste

⅓ cup shortening
¾ cup whole milk

2 cups all-purpose flour
2 tablespoons granulated sugar
3 teaspoons baking powder
1 teaspoon salt

1½ cups whipping cream
3 tablespoons granulated sugar
1 teaspoon pure vanilla extract

Mix strawberries and ⅔ cup sugar in a bowl; set aside.

Preheat oven to 450°.

Mix flour, 2 tablespoons sugar, baking powder and salt in a medium bowl.
Cut in shortening with a pastry blender or two knives until mixture resembles
fine crumbs. Stir in milk just until blended. Gently smooth dough into a ball on
a lightly floured pastry cloth. Knead 20–25 times. Do not over knead. Roll
dough to ½-inch thickness. Cut dough with a floured 3-inch biscuit cutter.
Place about 1 inch apart on an ungreased baking sheet. Bake until golden
brown, 10–12 minutes.

 Split cakes crosswise while hot. Spread with softened butter. Fill bottom
halves with strawberries and whipped cream. Add top halves; top with more
strawberries and whipped cream. Refrigerate leftovers.

Makes 6 servings.

COCONUT MACAROON
STRAWBERRY SHORTCAKE

Coconut lovers dream.

1⅓ cups sweetened flaked coconut
½ cup chopped slivered almonds
⅓ cup granulated sugar
2 tablespoons all-purpose flour
⅛ teaspoon salt

2 egg whites
½ teaspoon almond extract
1 cup thawed frozen nondairy whipped topping
2 cups fresh strawberries, sliced

Preheat oven to 325°.
Line a baking sheet with cooking foil; grease foil.

Mix coconut, almonds, sugar, flour and salt in a large bowl.

Beat egg whites and almond extract lightly with a fork in a small bowl; add to coconut mixture and mix well.

Spread coconut in a 9-inch circle onto prepared baking sheet (trace a 9-inch circle on foil before adding mixture). Bake until lightly browned, about 15–20 minutes. Remove from oven; cool. Remove from foil. Cut into wedges. Top evenly with whipped topping and strawberries just before serving. Refrigerate leftovers.

Makes 8 servings.

CREAM CHEESE STRAWBERRY SHORTCAKE

Creamy and delicious…and so easy to prepare.

2 cups all-purpose biscuit baking mix
2 tablespoons granulated sugar
½ cup butter or margarine, softened
⅓ cup warm water

1 8-ounce package cream cheese, softened
1 14-ounce can sweetened condensed milk
⅓ cup fresh lemon juice
1 teaspoon pure vanilla extract

1 quart fresh strawberries, hulled and sliced
1 16-ounce package prepared strawberry glaze, chilled
thawed nondairy whipped topping

Preheat oven to 400°.
Lightly grease a 9-inch square baking pan.

Mix biscuit baking mix and sugar in a small mixer bowl. Add butter and water; beat until well blended. Spoon mixture into prepared pan. Using floured hands, press dough evenly over bottom. Bake until lightly browned, about 10–12 minutes. Remove from oven; cool in pan.

Beat cream cheese in a large bowl with an electric mixer until fluffy. Gradually beat in sweetened condensed milk until smooth. Stir in lemon juice and vanilla extract. Spread evenly over cooled baked shortcake. Refrigerate and chill until set, at least 3 hours. Cut into squares.

Mix strawberries and glaze in a bowl; spoon over shortcake when serving. Garnish with thawed whipped topping as desired. Refrigerate leftovers.

Makes 8 servings.

MARY DOW'S STRAWBERRY-RHUBARB SHORTCAKES

Pretty easy…very tasty!

Sauce
⅔ cup granulated sugar
2 tablespoons cornstarch
¼ teaspoon ground ginger
¼ cup fresh orange juice
2 cups sliced fresh or frozen rhubarb
1½ cups fresh strawberries, hulled and halved
½ teaspoon pure vanilla extract

Shortcakes
8 individual sponge shortcake cups (purchased)
4 cups vanilla ice cream
sweetened whipped cream

Sauce: Mix sugar, cornstarch and ginger in a medium saucepan. Stir in orange juice until blended. Stir in rhubarb and strawberries. Bring mixture to a boil, stirring often. Reduce heat. Cook over medium-low heat until slightly thickened and rhubarb is soft, about 10 minutes. Remove from heat; stir in vanilla extract. Cool 10 minutes.

Shortcakes: Fill each cup with ½ cup ice cream. Spoon about ¼ cup strawberry-rhubarb sauce over each. Top with a dollop of whipping cream. Serve immediately. Refrigerate leftovers.

Makes 8 servings.

STRAWBERRY ALMOND CREAM SHORTCAKE

One-pan shortcake…a good choice.

Cake
½ cup butter, softened
½ cup granulated sugar
1 large egg
1 teaspoon almond extract
1½ cups all-purpose flour
½ teaspoon baking powder
½ cup sliced almonds, toasted

Filling
2 cups dairy sour cream
½ cup granulated sugar
2 eggs
1 teaspoon almond extract

Topping
2 cups fresh strawberries, halved
2 tablespoons strawberry jelly, melted

Preheat oven to 350°.
Grease a 9-inch springform pan.

Cake: Beat butter and ½ cup sugar in a large bowl on medium speed until creamy. Beat in egg and 1 teaspoon almond extract until blended. Reduce speed to low. Add flour and baking powder and continue beating until well mixed. Gently press dough onto bottom of prepared pan. Sprinkle almonds over dough; set aside.

Filling: Whisk all filling ingredients in a bowl until smooth. Pour mixture over almonds. Bake 60–70 minutes or until edges are lightly browned (surface of filling may crack). Cool completely in pan on a wire rack. Remove sides of pan.

Topping: Arrange strawberries in a circle on top of cake. Drizzle with melted jelly. Refrigerate and chill before serving. Refrigerate leftovers.

Makes 12 servings.

STRAWBERRY CHOCOLATE SHORTCAKE

Chocolate shortcake with strawberries…a special treat.

1 cup semi-sweet chocolate chips, divided
½ cup whole milk
2 cups all-purpose flour
2 tablespoons granulated sugar
1 tablespoon baking powder
1 teaspoon salt
½ cup butter

2 pints fresh strawberries, sliced mixed in a bowl with ¼ cup granulated sugar
sweetened whipped cream

Preheat oven to 450°.

Place ½ cup chocolate chips and milk in a saucepan over hot water (not boiling water). Stir until chocolate is melted and smooth; set aside.

Mix flour, 2 tablespoons sugar, baking powder and salt in a large bowl. Cut in butter with a pastry blender or 2 knives until mixture resembles coarse crumbs. Add chocolate mixture; stir until blended. Knead in remaining ½ cup chocolate chips. Roll dough out on a floured board to ½-inch thickness. Cut dough into 8 pieces with 3-inch round cookie cutter. Place on an ungreased baking sheet. Bake 8–10 minutes. Cool completely on a wire rack.

To serve, cut each short cake in half crosswise. Spoon bottom half with strawberries and plenty of whipped cream. Cover with top half. Spoon with more strawberries and whipped cream. Serve. Refrigerate leftovers.

Makes 8 servings.

STRAWBERRY SHORTCAKE SQUARES

An easy homemade cake to serve with strawberries and cream.

1¼ cups all-purpose flour
¾ cup granulated sugar
2½ teaspoons baking powder
½ teaspoon salt

⅔ cup whole milk
⅓ cup butter, softened
2 eggs
1 teaspoon pure vanilla extract

3 cups fresh strawberries mixed in a bowl with 2 tablespoons
   granulated sugar
1⅓ cups whipping cream whipped in a bowl with 3 tablespoons
   powdered sugar and 1 teaspoon pure vanilla extract

Preheat oven to 400°.
Grease an 8x8-inch square baking pan.

Mix flour, sugar, baking powder and salt in a medium bowl. Add milk, butter,
eggs and 1 teaspoon vanilla extract. Beat on medium speed, scraping bowl
often, until well mixed. Spread into prepared pan. Bake 25–30 minutes or
until lightly browned. Cool completely in pan on a wire rack. Cut into squares.

When serving, top each square generously with strawberries and whipped
cream. Refrigerate leftovers.

Makes 8 servings.

RHUBARB-STRAWBERRY COFFEECAKE

A cake mix is used in this streusel-topped cream cheese-glazed delight.

1 18.25-ounce package yellow
  cake mix, divided
⅔ cup brown sugar, packed
2 tablespoons cold butter
¾ cup chopped walnuts

2 large eggs
1 teaspoon pure vanilla extract
1 8-ounce container dairy sour cream
1½ cups finely chopped fresh rhubarb
1½ cups sliced fresh ripe strawberries

Glaze
**Beat 3 ounces softened cream cheese, ¾ cup powdered sugar, 1
tablespoon milk and ½ teaspoon pure vanilla extract in a bowl until
creamy and smooth.**

Preheat oven to 350°.
Grease a 13x9x2-inch baking pan.

Mix ⅔ cup dry cake mix and sugar in a large bowl. Cut in butter until crumbly.
Stir in walnuts; set aside.

Stir remaining cake mix, eggs, vanilla extract and sour cream in another
bowl. Fold in rhubarb and strawberries. Spread batter into prepared pan.
Sprinkle with reserved crumbly walnut mixture. Bake 40–50 minutes or
until a wooden pick inserted near center comes out clean. Cool in pan on
a wire rack. Drizzle glaze over cake. Refrigerate leftovers.

Makes 12 servings.

STRAWBERRY COFFEECAKE

Serve this tasty coffeecake warm for a special coffee break.

Cake
1 cup granulated sugar
½ cup butter, softened
1 cup dairy sour cream
2 eggs
1 teaspoon pure vanilla extract
2 cups all-purpose flour
1½ teaspoons baking powder
½ teaspoon baking soda
½ teaspoon salt
1 21-ounce can strawberry pie filling

Topping
¼ cup all-purpose flour
¼ cup granulated sugar
¼ cup chopped pecans
1 teaspoon ground cinnamon
3 tablespoons butter

Preheat oven to 325°.
Grease and flour a 13x9-inch baking pan.

Cake: Beat 1 cup sugar and ½ cup butter in a large bowl on medium speed until creamy. Beat in sour cream, eggs and vanilla extract until well mixed. Reduce speed to low. Beat in 2 cups flour, baking powder, baking soda and salt until well mixed. Spread half the batter into prepared pan. Spoon strawberry filling over batter. Carefully spread remaining batter over strawberry pie filling.

Topping: Mix ¼ cup flour, ¼ cup sugar, pecans and cinnamon in a medium bowl. Cut in 3 tablespoons butter until crumbly. Sprinkle mixture over batter. Bake 45–50 minutes or until a wooden pick inserted in center comes out clean. Refrigerate leftovers.

Makes 15 servings.

CREAMY COCONUT-FROSTED STRAWBERRY CUPCAKES

Strawberry cake mix is used in these easy to prepare coconut cream cheese frosted cupcakes.

Cupcakes
1 18.25-package strawberry cake mix
2 cups dairy sour cream
2 eggs
⅓ cup strawberry preserves

Frosting
1 8-ounce package cream cheese, softened

4 tablespoons butter, softened
1 teaspoon pure vanilla extract
½ cup sweetened coconut
3½ to 4 cups powdered sugar
½ cup mashed fresh strawberries, well drained

Preheat oven to 350°.

Cupcakes: Mix cake mix, sour cream and eggs in a large bowl. Stir with a spoon until well blended. Reserve ½ cup batter. Fill 24 paper-lined muffin cups half full with remaining batter.

Make a slight indentation in center of each with a spoon; fill with ½ teaspoon of strawberry preserves. Spoon remaining reserved batter evenly over preserves. Muffin cups should be three quarters full. Bake 20–30 minutes or until tops spring back when lightly touched in center. Cool in pan 1 minute; remove from pan and cool completely before frosting. Refrigerate.

Frosting: Beat cream cheese and butter in a medium bowl until fluffy. Gradually beat in powdered sugar, strawberries, vanilla extract and coconut until well blended. Frost cupcakes as desired. Refrigerate.

Makes 24 cupcakes.

PINK STRAWBERRY CUPCAKES

White cake mix is used in these pretty pink cupcakes. Garnish tops with fresh strawberry slices if desired.

Cupcakes
- 1 18.25-ounce package plain white cake mix
- 1 3-ounce package strawberry flavor gelatin
- 1 cup finely chopped fresh strawberries
- ¾ cup whole milk
- ¾ cup corn oil
- 1 teaspoon pure vanilla extract
- 4 large eggs

Frosting
- 1 8-ounce package cream cheese, softened
- 4 tablespoons butter
- 3 cups powdered sugar
- 1 teaspoon pure vanilla extract
- ½ cup mashed fresh strawberries, well drained

Preheat oven to 350°.
Paper-line two 12-cup muffin baking pans.

Cupcakes: Beat all cupcake ingredients in a mixer bowl with an electric mixer on low speed until blended. Beat on medium speed 2 minutes. Fill each muffin cup with batter three quarters full. Bake until lightly golden, about 20–25 minutes. Remove from oven; cool in pan on a rack 5 minutes. Remove from pan; cool completely on a wire rack before frosting.

Frosting: Beat cream cheese and butter on medium speed in a bowl until blended. Beat in sugar until well blended. Add vanilla extract and mashed strawberries; beat until fluffy. Frost cupcakes. Refrigerate leftovers.

Makes 24 cupcakes.

Tortes
Tarts

CHOCOLATE STRAWBERRY CREAMY TORTE

Pretty and tasty…top with small strawberries and powdered sugar.

Brownie
**1 19-5-ounce box fudge
  brownie mix**
½ cup corn oil
¼ cup water
3 eggs

Filling
1 8-ounce package cream cheese, softened

3 tablespoons granulated sugar
1 teaspoon pure vanilla extract
**1 6-ounce container thick and creamy
  strawberry yogurt**
1½ cups finely chopped fresh strawberries
½ cup heavy whipping cream
1½ cups semi-sweet chocolate chips

Preheat oven to 350°.
Spray bottoms of two 9-inch round cake pans with cooking spray.

Brownie: Prepare brownie mix as directed on box for cake-like brownies, using oil, water and eggs. Spread half of batter evenly in each prepared cake pan. Bake 18–23 minutes. Cool in pan on a wire rack 10 minutes. Remove from pans; cool completely on a wire rack.

Filling: Beat cream cheese, sugar and vanilla extract in a medium bowl on medium speed until well blended. Beat in yogurt until smooth. Fold in strawberries; refrigerate.

Fudge: Heat cream in a 1-quart saucepan over medium, stirring constantly, just until cream begins to boil. Immediately remove from heat. Add chocolate chips; press into cream. Cover and let stand 3 minutes. Beat with a wire whisk until smooth. Cool completely.

Place one brownie layer on a plate. Spread with half the strawberry mixture to within 1-inch of edge. Spread half the fudge almost to edge of the strawberry cream. Repeat layers. Immediately refrigerate. Chill well before serving. Cut into wedges with a hot knife. Refrigerate leftovers.

Makes 12 servings.

CHOCOLATE STRAWBERRY REFRIGERATOR TORTE

Chocolate filling and strawberries in a chocolate crust…yummy.

Crust
2 cups chocolate graham cracker crumbs
½ cup butter, melted
¼ cup granulated sugar

Filling
1 12-ounce container frozen nondairy whipped topping, thawed
1 cup dairy sour cream
1 3.9-ounce package instant chocolate pudding mix
2 cups fresh strawberries, sliced
1 ounce semi-sweet chocolate melted with 2 teaspoons butter;
  cool slightly

Crust: Mix all crust ingredients in a bowl. Press mixture onto bottom
and 1½-inches up sides of a greased 9-inch springform pan; refrigerate.

Filling: Beat whipped topping, sour cream and pudding mix in a large bowl until
blended. Spread half the mixture over prepared crust. Place strawberries over
top of pudding mixture. Spread remaining pudding mixture over strawberries.
Drizzle melted chocolate over top. Refrigerate and chill well, at least 5 hours,
before serving. Refrigerate leftovers.

Makes 10 servings.

STRAWBERRY CUSTARD TORTE

A cake mix is used in this luscious torte.

Crust
1 18.25-ounce package yellow
  cake mix

Filling
⅓ cup granulated sugar
1 tablespoon cornstarch
⅛ teaspoon salt
1 cup whole milk

2 egg yolks, lightly beaten in a small bowl
1 tablespoon butter
1 teaspoon pure vanilla extract

1 8-ounce container frozen non-dairy
  whipped topping, thawed
1 12-ounce package frozen sweetened
  sliced strawberries, thawed; drained

Prepare and bake cake following package directions using two greased
and floured 9-inch round cake pans. Cool 10 minutes. Remove from pans;
cool completely on a wire rack.

Filling: Mix sugar, cornstarch and salt in a medium saucepan. Gradually stir in
milk until smooth. Bring to a boil over medium heat. Cook, stirring constantly,
2 minutes or until thickened. Remove from heat. Stir a small amount of hot
filling into egg yolks, then return to pan, stirring constantly. Bring to a slow
boil; cook and stir 2 minutes. Remove from heat. Stir in butter and vanilla
extract. Cover and refrigerate until chilled.

Place half the whipped topping in a medium bowl. Fold in strawberries. Split
each cake layer into two horizontal layers. Spread with half of strawberry
mixture. Top with a second cake layer; spread with custard. Add a third cake
layer; spread with remaining strawberry mixture. Top with remaining cake
layer, then top with remaining whipped topping. Refrigerate 8 hours before
serving. Refrigerate leftovers.

Makes 12 servings.

APRICOT-GLAZED STRAWBERRY FRESH FRUIT TART

A creamy tart filled with fresh strawberries, kiwi, blueberries and raspberries in a baked buttery crust.

Crust
½ cup powdered sugar
1½ cups all-purpose flour
12 tablespoons butter, softened and cut into small pieces

Filling
1 8-ounce package cream cheese, softened
½ cup granulated sugar
1 teaspoon pure vanilla extract

½ cup whipping cream, whipped, divided
3 cups fresh strawberries, hulled and halved
1 kiwi, peeled and sliced
½ cup fresh blueberries
½ cup fresh raspberries

Glaze
½ cup apricot jam
1 tablespoon fresh lemon juice or water

Preheat oven to 350°.

Crust: Process all crust ingredients in a food processor until mixture forms a ball. Press dough in all indentations, using your fingers, into a 12-inch tart pan with removable bottom; pat until smooth. Bake 10–12 minutes or until lightly browned. Cool in pan on a wire rack.

Filling: Beat cream cheese in a bowl with an electric mixer until fluffy. Beat in sugar and vanilla extract until smooth. Fold in half of the whipped cream. Spread mixture over cooled crust. Arrange the strawberries in a circle over creamy mixture, then the kiwi, blueberries and raspberries.

Glaze: Heat apricot jam and lemon juice in a small saucepan until melted. Strain in a bowl and cool. Brush glaze over fruit. Refrigerate. Remove the side of pan and cut tart into wedges. Serve with remaining whipped cream as desired. Refrigerate leftovers.

Makes 8 servings.

CHOCOLATE CREAM STRAWBERRY TART

Chocolate cream and strawberries…a perfect pair.

pastry for one crust pie

Filling
¼ cup granulated sugar
3 tablespoons all-purpose flour
¼ teaspoon salt
1 cup whole milk

4 egg yolks, beaten in a bowl

1 cup semi-sweet chocolate chips
2 tablespoons butter
2 teaspoons pure vanilla extract
2 pints fresh strawberries
2 tablespoons strawberry jelly

Preheat oven to 425°.

Fit pastry dough into a 9-inch tart pan with removable bottom. Press dough firmly into bottom and sides of pan; trim edges. Line pastry dough with foil; weight with dried beans. Bake 10 minutes. Remove foil and beans. Bake 3 minutes. Cool completely. Remove from pan.

Filling: Mix sugar, flour and salt in a medium saucepan. Gradually add milk. Cook over low heat, stirring constantly, until mixture boils. Boil 2 minutes, stirring constantly. Remove from heat; stir a small amount of hot mixture into beaten eggs, then return all to saucepan and beat until well blended. Cook and stir 1 minute. Remove from heat.

Add butter, chocolate chips and vanilla extract. Stir until chocolate is melted and mixture is smooth. Place food plastic wrap over mixture; chill 30 minutes. Stir mixture and spread evenly into baked tart shell. Arrange strawberries on top. Melt strawberry jelly in a small saucepan over low heat; brush over strawberries. Chill tart several hours. Let stand at room temperature 15 minutes before serving. Refrigerate leftovers.

Makes 8 servings.

GLAZED STRAWBERRY-BANANA TART

A pat-in-the-pan crust makes this tart easy to prepare.

Crust
1½ cups all-purpose flour
¾ cup butter
⅓ cup powdered sugar
¼ teaspoon salt

½ cup orange marmalade
2 tablespoons orange juice

Filling
1 cup dairy sour cream
1 cup whole milk
1 4-serving size package instant vanilla pudding and pie mix
4 cups fresh strawberries
1 ripe banana, sliced

Preheat oven to 400°.

Crust: Mix all crust ingredients in a bowl with your hands until crumbly. Press mixture firmly onto bottom of an ungreased 11-inch tart pan with removable bottom. Bake until light brown, about 8–10 minutes. Cool completely in pan on a wire rack. Remove side from pan.

Filling: Beat sour cream, milk and dry pudding mix on low speed in a mixer bowl 1–2 minutes or until blended; spread mixture over crust.

Top with strawberries and banana slices. Heat marmalade and orange juice in a small saucepan until melted. Cool slightly and spoon over strawberries and banana slices. Serve. Refrigerate leftovers.

Makes 12 servings.

KIWIFRUIT AND STRAWBERRY TART

An easy to make buttery crust holds this delectable tart.
Hint: Use a 12-inch pizza pan if you don't have a tart pan.

Crust
⅓ cup granulates sugar
½ cup butter softened
1¼ cups all-purpose flour
2 tablespoons whole milk
½ teaspoon pure vanilla extract

Filling
1 cup dairy sour cream
1 tablespoon granulated sugar
½ teaspoon pure vanilla extract

Topping
2 kiwifruit, peeled and sliced
2 cups strawberries, sliced

Preheat oven to 400°.

Crust: Beat ⅓ cup sugar and butter in a large mixer bowl on medium speed until creamy, about 2 minutes. Beat in flour, milk and ½ teaspoon vanilla extract on low speed until well mixed. Press dough onto bottom and up sides of a 10-inch tart pan with removable bottom. Prick dough all over with a fork. Bake until light golden brown 14–20 minutes. Cool completely in pan on a wire rack.

Filling: Stir all filling ingredients in a bowl; spread over cooled crust.

Topping: Arrange fruit on top of filling. Serve or store immediately in the refrigerator. Refrigerate leftovers.

Makes 10 servings.

LEMON-STRAWBERRY TART

Substitution: Use a 12-ounce jar purchased lemon curd for filling.

Crust
1¼ cups all-purpose flour
1 tablespoon granulated sugar
¼ teaspoon salt
½ cup cold butter
1 egg yolk, beaten
2–3 tablespoons cold water

Filling
⅔ cup granulated sugar
4 teaspoons cornstarch
¼ cup fresh lemon juice
¼ cup water
3 egg yolks, beaten in a bowl
¼ cup butter

Topping
3 cups sliced fresh ripe strawberries
1 tablespoon red currant jelly, melted

Preheat oven to 425°.

Crust: Mix flour, 1 tablespoon sugar and salt in a medium bowl. Cut in butter until mixture resembles coarse crumbs. Add 1 egg yolk. Stir in enough water with a fork just until flour is moistened. Form dough into a ball. Roll dough between two pieces of waxed paper to an 11-inch square. Remove paper. Press dough into an ungreased 9-inch square tart pan with a removable bottom. Trim excess. Prick bottom and sides with a fork. Bake 15–18 minutes or until lightly browned. Cool completely.

Filling: Mix ⅔ cup sugar and cornstarch in a 1-quart saucepan. Stir in lemon juice and ¼ cup water. Cook over medium-high heat, stirring constantly, until mixture comes to a boil, about 2–3 minutes. Remove from heat. Stir half of hot mixture into egg yolks. Return all to saucepan. Cook and stir over low heat until mixture boils and thickens. Remove from heat. Stir in ¼ cup butter. Place plastic food wrap on surface of filling. Refrigerate at least 1 hour. Spread chilled filling into crust.

Topping: Arrange strawberries on chilled filling in crust. Drizzle with melted jelly just before serving. Refrigerate leftovers.

Makes 9 servings.

MASCARPONE TART WITH FRESH STRAWBERRIES

Pretty and delicious…top with a dollop of whipped cream if desired.

Crust
**2 cups finely crushed chocolate
  wafer cookie crumbs**
½ cup melted butter
2 tablespoons granulated sugar
2 teaspoons instant espresso powder

Topping
powdered sugar
2 cups fresh strawberries thinly sliced just before serving

Filling
**16-ounces mascarpone or cream
  cheese**
⅓ cup honey
1 teaspoon pure vanilla extract
2 large eggs
2 tablespoons all-purpose flour
¼ teaspoon salt

Preheat oven to 325°.

Crust: Mix all crust ingredients in a bowl; press mixture evenly onto bottom and up sides of a 10-inch tart pan with removable bottom. Place pan on a rimmed baking sheet; set aside.

Filling: Beat cheese, honey and vanilla extract with an electric mixer on medium speed until smooth. Beat in eggs. Beat in flour and salt. Pour mixture into prepared crust. Bake until filling is barely set in center, about 30–35 minutes. Remove from oven; cool in pan on a rack 30 minutes, then immediately refrigerate and chill at least 1 hour.

Topping: Place strawberries on tart in an overlapping circular pattern. Dust strawberries with powdered sugar as desired. Refrigerate leftovers.

Makes 10 servings.

RHUBARB-STRAWBERRY TART

Rhubarb and strawberries…a perfect pairing. Top each serving with whipped cream if desired.

Crust
½ (15-ounce) package refrigerated pie dough

Filling
2 cups sliced fresh rhubarb
½ cup granulated sugar
2 tablespoons cornstarch
½ teaspoon ground cinnamon
2 teaspoons water

3 cups fresh strawberries, sliced
1 teaspoon pure vanilla extract

1 tablespoon granulated sugar mixed in a cup with ¼ teaspoon ground cinnamon

Preheat oven to 400°.

Crust: Press dough onto bottom and up sides of a 10-inch tart pan with removable bottom. Line bottom of dough with foil; top foil with pie weights or dried beans. Bake 5 minutes. Remove foil and weights. Bake another 5 minutes. Cook on a wire rack.

Filling: Mix rhubarb, ½ cup sugar, cornstarch, cinnamon and water in a saucepan. Bring to a boil; reduce heat and simmer until rhubarb is tender, stirring often, about 5 minutes. Remove from heat. Stir in strawberries and vanilla. Spoon mixture into prepared crust. Sprinkle with sugar-cinnamon. Place tart on a baking sheet. Bake about 30 minutes or until filling is set. Cool on a wire rack. Refrigerate leftovers.

Makes 8 servings.

SAM'S CHOCOLATE CREAM STRAWBERRY TART

Chocolate cream and strawberries...like Sam, unforgettable.

Tart Shell
pastry for one 9-inch pie

Filling
¼ cup granulated sugar
3 tablespoons all-purpose flour
¼ teaspoon salt
1 cup whole milk
4 egg yolks, beaten in a small bowl

1 cup semi-sweet chocolate chips
2 tablespoons butter
2 teaspoons vanilla extract

Topping
2 pints fresh strawberries
2 tablespoons strawberry jelly
sweetened whipped cream

Preheat oven to 425°.

Shell: Press dough onto bottom and up sides of an ungreased 9-inch tart pan with removable bottom; trim edges. Line dough with foil and add dried beans (to weigh down). Bake 10 minutes. Remove foil and beans. Bake 2–3 more minutes. Cool completely. Remove shell from pan.

Filling: Mix sugar, flour and salt in a medium saucepan. Gradually stir in milk. Cook over low heat, stirring constantly, until mixture boils. Boil 2 minutes, stirring constantly. Beat a small amount hot filling mixture in egg yolks; return all to saucepan. Stir and cook 2 minutes longer. Remove from heat. Stir in chocolate chips, butter and vanilla until smooth. Cover with plastic food wrap. Chill 30 minutes. Stir; spread into baked tart shell.

Topping: Top chilled filling with strawberries, pointed ends up. Melt jelly in a small saucepan over low heat; brush over strawberries. Refrigerate and chill. Let stand at room temperature 15 minutes when serving. Top with whipped cream. Refrigerate leftovers.

Makes 8 servings.

S'MORE STRAWBERRY TART

A tart that is sure to bring requests for s'more!

Crust
1 cup graham cracker crumbs
¼ cup granulated sugar
¼ cup butter, melted

Filling
⅔ cup whipping cream
10-ounces semi-sweet chocolate, chopped

1½ cups thinly sliced fresh strawberries
½ cup marshmallow creme
8 whole strawberries, cleaned and hulled

Preheat oven to 350°.

Crust: Mix all crust ingredients in a bowl. Press mixture onto bottom and up sides of a 9-inch tart pan with removable bottom. Bake 8 minutes. Cool completely. Place on a baking sheet; set aside.

Filling: Heat whipping cream in a medium saucepan over low heat until bubbles form around edge of pan. Remove from heat. Add chocolate; cook, stirring constantly, over low heat until melted. Remove from heat; cool to lukewarm, about 5 minutes.

Place strawberry slices in single layer in crust. Pour melted chocolate mixture over strawberries. Microwave marshmallow creme in a microwave-safe bowl 30 seconds or until softened. Stir just until smooth. Immediately drop by spoonfuls over chocolate layer. Swirl into chocolate with the tip of a knife. Place 8 whole strawberries around edge of tart. Refrigerate until chocolate is set, about 1 hour. Refrigerate leftovers.

Makes 8 servings.

About the Author

Theresa Millang is a popular and versatile cookbook author. She has written successful cookbooks on muffins, brownies, pies, cookies, cheesecake, casseroles, and several on Cajun cooking. She has cooked on television and contributed many recipes to food articles throughout the U.S.A.

Theresa's Other Cookbooks
I Love Cheesecake
I Love Pies You Don't Bake
The Muffins Are Coming

Theresa's Other Current Cookbooks
The Best of Cajun-Creole Recipes
The Best of Chili Recipes
The Great Minnesota Hot Dish
The Joy of Apples
The Joy of Blueberries
The Joy of Cherries
The Joy of Cranberries
The Joy of Rhubarb